IT'S NOT YOUR LIFE, IT'S YOU

A LAYMAN'S GUIDE TO THE POWER OF PERSPECTIVE

JASON KENDRICK

IT'S NOT YOUR LIFE,
IT'S YOU

This edition published 2010 by It's You Publishing
Texas, USA

First Edition

Copyright 2009 © Jason Kendrick
The moral right of the author has been asserted.

It's You Publishing
210 Wall Dr.
Palestine,
TX 75803

All rights reserved. No part of this publication may be reproduced, stored in or introduced into a retrieval system, or transmitted, in any form, or by any means (electronic, mechanical, photocopying, recording or otherwise) without the prior written permission of the copyright owner.

ISBN 978 0 557 72361 4

Printed and bound in USA by
Lightning Source Printing
www.lightningsource.com
1246 Heil Quaker Blvd.
La Vergne, TN USA 37086

CONTENTS

ACKNOWLEDGMENTS — 5

INTRODUCTION — 9

CHAPTER 1: — 19
MENTALITY = REALITY!

CHAPTER 2: — 43
WHO AND WHAT YOU REALLY ARE!

CHAPTER 3: — 62
NOTHING IS BAD AND BAD IS NOTHING!

CHAPTER 4: — 78
YOU CHOSE THIS LIFE!

CHAPTER 5: — 89
LISTEN TO YOU!

CHAPTER 6: — 104
HAPPINESS COMES FROM WITHIN!

CHAPTER 7: — 114
SIMPLICITY IS BLISS!

CHAPTER 8: — 125
GOD BELIEVES IN YOU.

CHAPTER 9: — 134
HELP YOURSELF, BY GETTING OUT OF THE WAY!

CHAPTER 10: — 144
SO, WHAT DOES THIS ALL MEAN FOR YOU?

EPILOGUE — 148

ACKNOWLEDGEMENTS

I would like to take this opportunity to thank all of those who have come into my life to teach me the lessons I had to learn to get to this point. I hope you all know who you are, because I'd have to write another book just to thank you all individually. I would also like to take this opportunity to go ahead and thank all of those who will come into my life in the future to help me learn my new lessons on this ever-evolving adventure that is my life. I hope that I will learn the grace that I didn't have before, to appreciate you in the moment, and not just in hindsight, as I have so many times in my past.

First and foremost I would like to thank my Mom and Dad for bringing me into this world and for being the perfect examples I needed. Mom, a special thank you to you for helping me to finally finish the editing process and for being my 'A' number '1' financier while getting this first book out.

To Patrice Delanty and Mary Redford; for being willing to put in the time and effort as the first to read and begin the editing process for this manuscript. Your help and insight are greatly appreciated!

To Dannion Brinkley, for being the supportive, encouraging and wonderful example to me that he was and still is to this day; and for letting me 'borrow' some of your favorite material to use in this book, thank you, oh GREAT AND MIGHTY SPIRITUAL BEING WITH DIGNITY, DIRECTION AND PURPOSE. To the rest of the Peters-Brinkley clan; Kathryn, Elizabeth, Alix, Evan, Alysia, Angel and Adrianna, thank you for accepting me into your home and into your family, the lessons I received and Love I felt was more appreciated than you will ever know.

To my friend, CSL partner, movie / Ihop buddy and first official life coaching client, Crystal Starlight, you have been the greatest friend, wonderful example, and inspiration to me during our friendship and work together. (You're Big Time, Baby!)

To all of my Colorado friends from Breckenridge, Denver and parts in between, I love you all and couldn't have made it without each and every one of you.

To Alan, who I met standing in line to go see Dannion speak for the first time, thank you for suggesting that I write a book. I know that you were a messenger for God whether you knew it, remember it or not.

Last, but not least, to all my other family, friends, acquaintances and coworkers from all over the world, thank you for all of your influence and love!

We'll see you in book two....And three and four... ☺

INTRODUCTION

Good day to you or whatever it may be for you now. I would like to take this opportunity to thank you for picking up this book and taking a chance with it. I surmise that someone else told you about this book or possibly the title intrigued you. Either way, I can guarantee that you will get something of value from what is written here, whether it is a strengthening of your own thoughts and opinions, verification of what you have already been thinking and feeling, or entirely new ideas.

In any case, it will be useful. ☺

The ideas and opinions expressed in this book are not intended to promote or discourage any particular religious belief or dogma. However, I would like to think that what I present to you will strengthen your connection to God, The Source, The Is, or whatever terminology you prefer. The more that I learn about this life and my other lives, past and future, the closer my bond / connection to The Source is and the better and happier I feel about my current life. My only wish is to spread a little of that to as many of you as possible.

I do realize that the ideas, theories and truths presented in this book may seem far-fetched and hard to swallow for some. This is as it should be. We are all on our own path and all points on our respective spiritual journeys resonate with different teachings and truths. It is not possible for everyone on this earth to think and act exactly the same and even if it were, how boring would that be, to have everyone thinking and doing the same things. The order of the universe is far too complex for most of us to even fathom, but to put it in the simplest terms possible will work well for our purposes here.

Everything and everyone has a plan, a place and a purpose; good, bad, or indifferent. Everything is a part of this big machine called life.

When we look at the world and our own lives in this way, it is much more likely we will find a bit of solace and peace. Now, to twist your noodle a bit more, try this one on for size: *You chose this life to live before you were born!*

Now you just have to figure out why; and here's a hint: *It usually has to do with what you will learn, have learned, or need to learn to progress in your spiritual growth.*

To all of you spiritually enlightened souls out there devouring all the self-help spiritual texts you can get your hands on (and I have been there), I have this to say to you: *Until you figure out your lesson and path for this life, you don't know squat!*

OH, AND ONE MORE THING --

Just living your life to live it is just as good a reason to be alive as trying to save the world and everyone in it. And just in case you're wondering, the world doesn't need saving! It is just fine! People merely want to be reminded of who they really are, what they once knew and have forgotten and want to remember again.

How did I come to know these things? Let's start with a little background about my life to this point.

BIOGRAPHY

My name is Jason Kendrick, and at the time I write this my age is 32. I was born to a military family in October 1975 at an Army Hospital located on the Fort Riley Army Post, Kansas, US of A. I don't remember much of Kansas or more correctly anything at all. After six months at Fort Riley, my father was sent to Wurzburg, Germany and off we all went with him. And this is pretty much how things went for the rest of my childhood: Kansas to Germany, Germany to Texas, Texas to Georgia, Georgia back to Texas, Texas back to Germany, and Germany to Alabama.

I graduated in 1994 from Sparkman High School in northern Alabama. During my last year of High School I signed up for the delayed enlistment program for the US Air Force, and after graduation it was back to Texas for basic training and technical school. I became an F-16 Weapons Troop and was stationed at Spangdahlem Airbase, Spangdahlem, Germany. Yes, back to Germany again. I am a lucky guy, what can I say?

This part of my life was a good time, full of lots of fun and travel. My squadron did tours in Turkey, Tunisia, Sardignia, and many other places I didn't get a chance to go. This was also a time of great learning and growing for me. I did not finish my full tour of duty due some indiscretions on my part. What can I say? I was young and stupid; but the lessons I learned during that time have been invaluable to me.

It is important to look back at the previous times of our lives so that we may consider all that was and all that transpired, whether pleasant or not, and realize what we learned from what happened. This will make you feel much better about the rough times of your life when you look at them as positive in this way.

After my dismissal from the Air Force, I bounced around from job to job for a few years until I began to question why I was still living in Northern Alabama. As lovely a place as it was, it did not suit me anymore. So I left with a good friend of mine and ended up in Breckenridge Colorado. At the time, it was the perfect place for me. I taught snowboarding and lived the mountain town lifestyle at full speed ahead. I have to say I definitely had a good time during this period of my life.

I indulged myself as much as I could, and in doing so I learned I wanted a change in my life. I met a wonderful girl and learned much from her and our relationship. Though, I do believe it was more from the mistakes I made and the pain those mistakes caused the two of us that I really learned the most. I am very grateful to her and to that relationship for all that it taught me and for the action it spurred within me. (Thank you, Iveta).

After about 6 years living in that little mountain party town, I made a change and moved 70 miles to the east to Denver, Colorado. It was in Denver that I really began to explore who and what I really am. I learned that I am an Indigo adult and a natural healer. As a result, I've studied Reiki and other types of hands on healing. I am also developing my innate psychic abilities at the Inner Insight Institute, which was modeled after the Berkeley Psychic Institute in Berkeley California.

It was during my first Metaphysical Fair that I was introduced to the notion of Indigos and that I might be a part of that group. Here is a description of Indigos so that you may understand what this means to me and other Indigos.

INDIGOS

Indigos have very unique characteristics that set them apart from previous generations. The name itself indicates the Life Color they carry in their auras and is indicative of the Third Eye Chakra, which represents intuition and psychic ability. As children these are usually the ones who are often rebellious to authority, nonconformist, extremely emotionally and sometimes physically sensitive or fragile, highly talented or academically gifted and often metaphysically gifted as well, usually intuitive, very often labeled ADD, either very empathic and compassionate OR very cold and callous, and are wise beyond their years. Indigos have come into this world with difficult challenges to overcome. Their extreme levels of sensitivity are hard to understand and appreciate by parents who don't share this trait. The Indigos are the ones who have come to raise the vibration of our planet! These are the primary ones who will bring us the enlightenment to ascend.

Wendy H. Chapman

It was with this description and through my continued study of Indigo, Crystal, and Rainbow Children that I began to really understand myself, and began to appreciate my true calling. As I looked back over my life and talked with my parents about my childhood, it became even more clearly evident that I am an Indigo. I am here as a guide, a teacher, and a healer. I am here to once again speak my truth and to help as many people as possible remember who they truly are.

More and more people are ready to remember that they are not defined by their bodies or this life. More people everyday are remembering on their own that they are more; that they are powerful spiritual beings who have bravely come forth to this physical realm to create through their thoughts and actions. We are the creators. It requires one of us to take the information from the universe and bring it into physical reality. In our natural spiritual forms we cannot create. We may know all things, but we cannot create any of it, which is why we are here: *To Create!*

How does that relate to being an Indigo, and what does that means to you? Well, let's just say that what I know I didn't get from any textbook or online college course. I have, what I like to call "an open connection" to Source, which means I get my information directly from my guides, angels, ancestors, Source, God, or whatever you would like to call it.

I know, I know. This sounds like a really cool thing doesn't it? Well, be careful what you wish for. I've had hard times due to this in the past, trying to explain things to others that I "just knew" and yet had absolutely no physical evidence or backing for, can be difficult. But as much as I knew the sky was blue just like the ocean, I knew these things.

Oh, and try this on for size: Try having all of this Source knowledge being pumped into your head, with no real sense of what to do with it while living in this world of rules, regulations, and religions. It can be a bit of a nightmare trying to rationally discuss things with those who are totally convinced that what they have been told is the "be-all and end-all" of all things.

I like to approach these folks very carefully indeed, and just suggest the evolution of knowledge has not been completed yet. We know now that the world is not flat, nor is it the center of our solar system. And so shall we know that we are eternal spiritual beings, living in this physical time-space reality, and that we create our own reality as we see fit.

I do not claim absolute knowledge or pretend to be a guide to the new millennium. I am only a thinker of differing thoughts, just like many of you, and have found them to be very beneficial to me throughout my life. It is these thoughts and points of view I share with you here, in hopes to inspire some, perhaps enrage others, but always to make you think.

My only request in our little adventure together is this: Please take everything you read here only for whatever value it has for you. Meaning, all of us in the physical realm are exactly where we need to be, and want to be, in our spiritual growth and experience. None of you will respond the same to what is written here. Nor will all of you agree with everything I have written.

This is as it should be. The fact that you have this book in your hands now tells me that you are ready to read these words. You are ready in one fashion or another to read what is written here, whether it be to inspire you to a new way of life, or just to use this book as kindling in your fire place. Either way, it will be of some use to you. However, all humor aside, merely judge for yourself what is written here for what it is, and how it resonates with you; that is all I ask.

Now, let us begin.

MENTALITY = REALITY

CHAPTER ONE

Let me start off first by saying, as with most things in life, this chapter will be the easiest to understand and the hardest to master. So, I have placed it first in the book, first and foremost to get your attention, but also so that those of you who never make it much past the first three chapters of any book will get the good stuff up front.

Mentality equals reality. Period, the end, put a fork in me, I'm done, end of story! Easy, Right?!

What do you mean, you want more? Need more explanation? You don't really need anything more than that -- it is all right there for you: Mentality equals reality. Doesn't that sum it up so perfectly?

Yes, of course it does, and yet, no, it really doesn't at all. Many of you may be thinking; "Oh lord, not another one of these 'wannabe mystical masters' talking in riddles again!" Have no fear! I wouldn't dream of leaving you out in the cold like that. I just like to keep it light and fun. As a wise man once said, "If you're not laughing, you're not doing it right!" Now those are words to live by! Well, that is, if you ask me.

Simply put, how and what you think determines your reality and your life. If you are a "woe-is-me" sort of person, I can imagine that you may have a life filled with difficulty, where nothing seems to go right; day-in and day-out, one disaster after another. Or maybe you know someone like this: all they seem to do is complain, and all they seem to get is more things to complain about. Ever wonder why?

Now on the other side, I am sure you know some people who are fearless and outgoing; they seem to have an endless stream of good luck and good fortune, and they talk about it all the time; saying things like: "My life is great! I am truly blessed! I am lucky, I win things all the time!" And so on. You know people like this right? And, you probably hate their guts, don't you? You just can't stand that guy with his wonderful life, strutting around seemingly shoving it into everyone's face and making them feel worse about their lives!! Right? Am I Right? Well, get over it. He is no more shoving his life in your face than you are justified in hating him for having a good one.

Oh, and did I mention I'm going to show you how to have a life even better than that guy's? Well, I am.

If you go back and read over that first part, you may notice a similarity in the two examples I gave to you. That similarity is that they both were right about their lives and situations.

They both knew how their lives were and how they would go; and surprisingly enough they were right. This is something I would like you to think about for a while. Save your place, put this book down and just ponder that for awhile. They knew how their lives were and would be; and they were right. Their lives turned out exactly like they predicted. Ponder that again for a moment.

> *"Whether you think you can or you think you can't, you're right!"*
>
> **- Henry Ford**

Mentality equals reality.

What do I mean by this? And, more particularly, what does it mean to you?

Whatever you think about yourself, your life, and the situations you run into every day, you are probably right. The problem is, the majority of us think very negatively. We think about what is wrong far more than we think about what is right. We complain about what we don't like about ourselves and other people and our society, whether it is money, religion, politics, relationships, kids, family, and on and on and on. It is amazing to me that this is how we basically think in our culture today.

What is really amazing to me is how habitual it is, and how hard it is to break the cycle. It is a constant battle to remain positive and to think positively, which is why I said in the beginning that this is the easiest concept to understand, but the hardest to master. Thankfully, as with any new skill, the more you practice, the easier it gets.

Changing how we think about things, our outlook on those things and the people in our day-to-day lives can actually change the world we live in. The idea is to change your world, your own personal little universe, first. Make yourself happy and joyous, and let the rest just fall into place. It is from our example, that we create the most change in the world.

"Our deepest fear is not that we are inadequate. Our deepest fear is that we are powerful beyond measure. It is our light, not our darkness that most frightens us. We ask ourselves, 'Who am I to be brilliant, gorgeous, talented, fabulous?' Actually, who are you not to be? You are a child of God. Your playing small does not serve the world. There is nothing enlightened about shrinking so that other people won't feel insecure around you. We are all meant to shine, as children do. We were born to make manifest the glory of God that is within us. It's not just in some of us; it's in everyone. And as we let our own light shine, we unconsciously give other people permission to do the same.

As we are liberated from our own fear, our presence automatically liberates others."

- **Marianne Williamson**

How can I change my life? How can I lead by example?

First, change your thinking. Stop all of the 'NO's in your life. Stop living a life in which all you do is shout 'NO' at the things you don't want. Shouting 'NO' at something has never made it go away; it **only** brings it closer to you. This is a fundamental law of the universe. This is the only fundamental law of the universe. ATTRACTION. We attract what we see every day by our thoughts, actions and attitudes. The universe has great faith in us and always brings us what we are thinking about and focusing on. Yelling "NO" at something does not tell the universe not to bring it to you. The universe only hears what it is you are thinking about and focused on. For example, yelling "NO" at traffic only magnetizes you to traffic; yelling "NO," at debt, only magnetizes you to debt, and so on.

Here is another example:

How many times have you been dreading something, and all of your thoughts about that thing are negative? How many times did that event or thing live up (or down) to your negative expectations? Most of the time, I would hazard to guess.

Now, how many times did you look forward to something? Something that you were longing for, for quite a long time and how great was that experience? Did the world seem to open up and bestow upon you unlimited joy and energy?

It is amazing how often these things occur and how many experiences we have that completely relate to our thoughts and expectations. Yet, do we notice? Not usually. We prefer to just call it 'Murphy's Law' or 'The Way of The World' or whatever favorite rationalization we may like to use.

These are very simple and broad examples, but they do illustrate the point, and most of you can probably relate to them in one fashion or another. To some, they may seem farfetched and fantastical, but with a little bit of thought about your past, I am certain that many of your experiences will resonate with the truth of what I've written here.

Now, on to the good stuff: Let's get into the hows and whys of this thing. Hopefully, you are starting to realize the power you have to change your life, and that you are the creator of your personal universe. But, you may be asking, how does this work? What do I do with this new information and new way of thinking?

There are many, many, many ways to effect change in your life. There are as many varied methods as there are countries, languages, religions, and people. I will give you a few of my methods and thoughts; try them out and see how they work for you. Then go out and learn yourself; try a new method. Keep learning and trying until you have enough knowledge and experience to create your own personal method that works in your own personal universe.

There are similarities to every method and every rationale

when related to the "mentality affecting your reality" concept. Truth is truth. But, method is method, and we all have different ways of doing the same thing. So don't get frustrated if someone else's method doesn't work for you. However, something in that method made sense to you and at least caused a change in how you react to the world. Take that and use it and then go find more and more things that resonate and work for you.

I am only a guide and assistant to you. You are the captain of your ship; and only you can make the final decisions about your life. Whether you call me your "first mate," "your right hand man," or for those Trekkies out there, your "number one," whatever you like is fine with me. Just learn and grow and create your universe however YOU see fit.

STEP ONE: KNOW THYSELF

You will have to be open and honest with yourself. As humans, we have a great capacity to delude ourselves and rationalize away anything we do not particularly like. Honesty with one's self is much like the first step of a 12-step program, which is to admit that you have a problem in the first place. Also, admitting that you are human and may not like to take responsibility for yourself or your life is the first step to turning your life around and truly making it better.

I have learned that I am the creator and master of my universe. Which means that whatever I bring into my universe is ultimately my fault and my responsibility; this is true for all of us. Every last person on this earth lives in their own world, of their own creation.

Many of you may have just had a visceral reaction to this concept, so let me explain further. There may be 6 billion people living on this spinning ball of dirt and water we call Earth; however, each person lives in their own world, their own reality. We all live in our own world, made up of our experiences. Yes, we can say that we all live in the same world, or more correctly, on the same world; but, none of us have had the exact same experiences, nor do we see the exact same things, react exactly the same to things, or love, like, dislike or hate the exact same things. Even identical twins have their own unique personalities and unique experiences.

Now that you are getting a grasp of this concept, try this on for size: since you are the only one in your individual world having your experiences and living your life, then it is reasonable to say that only you are responsible for your life and your experiences. Similarly, you are the only one you need to convince to change your life and your experiences. You do not need anyone else to help you to change your life. All you need to do is change your own mind, your own outlook, and your own expectations; and the rest will fall into place before you.

"The only thing in the world that we have control over, and I mean real control, not imagined or rationalized control is how we react to the people, experiences and things in our lives. You cannot control others in any way shape or form. No matter how

much you think or believe you can, you cannot. The only aspect to life that is totally and emphatically under our control is how we react to the world. How you react to the world is the easiest, best, and only way to affect change in your life immediately. Simply be aware of your reactions. Replace negative reactions with positive or indifferent reactions. Jesus said to turn the other cheek. This is what I believe he meant."

If you want to lose weight, then convince yourself that you will lose weight. Know that you will be, and are the perfect weight; and you will look the way you desire to look. Focus only on the outcome. Put up pictures of people who look how you want to look, and focus on seeing yourself looking that way. Do not focus on the action of losing weight. That will only keep you on a perpetual cycle of needing to lose weight. Focus ONLY on the end result until it makes itself into a reality.

No matter what others say or do, it is only up to you whether you do the things you want to do or not. If you are truly determined to lose weight and be healthier, then you will attract those people, places and events into your life that will create the new slimmer, stronger, and healthier body you desire.

And here is a big bonus for you all: You don't have to completely change your life or rearrange everything. The simple act of deciding the outcome you want and knowing within yourself that no matter what else happens this will be your outcome will make it so. The universe, your world, your life, will simply fall into place with the new you. Those things that encouraged you to be unhealthy and overweight will disappear, and all of the things that encourage you to be healthier and slimmer and more active will simply take the place of those other influences.

No matter what it is in the world that you want to be or to change, the power is within you. Change your mind and you change your life.

There are examples of this permeating the world we live upon today. I must admit -- one of my favorite television shows, and a guilty pleasure of mine, is "Driven," a program on MTV and VH1. Every story of a musician or an actor in that show has one main theme in common; They believed without a shadow of a doubt that they would 'make it' and did not stop until they did -- even after they 'made it'. They were told "NO," at every turn, but they just held on to their vision and kept moving. Until finally, someone of vision saw the potential that the artist saw within themselves, and in turn gave them the opportunity to succeed.

"More often than not, it is not about convincing others of who you are, but convincing yourself and changing your own mind. Then, it is a matter of

knowing yourself and being you for the world to see. As you know yourself, and are yourself in every action, you will inspire by example. Show others that you are a GREAT, WONDERFUL, and POWERFUL spiritual / human being by letting your inner light shine. They will have no choice but to acknowledge you for who you are--because that is who you truly are. Thus, by convincing yourself, you convince everyone else."

No matter what others say to you, if you know it and you believe it, you can create it and live it. However, I need to add one little disclaimer that relates to what I said previously: You must take step one, "be honest with yourself and take responsibility for yourself", before you can move forward to change your life.

These are wonderful examples of how life works. Another good example of those who break rule number one, are the contestants on American Idol. I applaud those who will not take 'NO' for an answer and are striving to better themselves. BUT, and this is a big BUT, you must know yourself before you strive for something. Most things in life are easy and you only need to change your own mind and take action. Many others are reliant upon popular opinion.

What this means is that if you are not a singer or a performer, do not try to be one. There are numerous things that you are good at and excel at. Stick with those things and you will be much more pleased with the results. Besides, you need to be careful what you wish for. You may think you want that fame and stardom, until you achieve it and it turns out to be nothing like you imagined it to be. That is why I say, be honest with yourself and stick to what talents you do have.

True happiness and Heaven on Earth comes from knowing yourself and doing what you love. And, thankfully, that is different for every person on the planet. Even those that make millions doing the same sport or using similar talents are different from each other. Embrace your difference and run with it. This will make you happy beyond your wildest dreams.

STEP TWO: BE PERSISTENT AND UNWAVERING

This step is where most people start to lose their way and fall off the "self-help / improve-your-life" wagon. You must be persistent and unwavering in your conviction to affect change and get what you are striving for. You must know and hold to the outcome of your desires and let nothing and no one dissuade you from reaching that goal.

Our physical life is about contrast. It is the contrasts of this world that create desires within you and spurs you to action. You see or experience something you do not care for, and that creates a desire for something different and better. This is the "yin and yang" of life.

We are completely capable of living a perfectly joyous and fulfilling life. Yet, even in achieving such a life, we will see contrasts that create desires within us. If you do not like the contrasts in your life, change it. Isolate yourself and do not interact with anyone else. Live your life totally free of interactions of any kind. This will allow you to maintain that joyous perfect state you live in, and may well drive you stark raving mad from boredom and lack of stimulus.

The idea is not to condemn these contrasts in our lives and what we see in the world, but to rejoice in them. Change how you react to things in the world; that is the only thing that you control anyway. Look at something that is in contrast with where you are and celebrate it, for it has created desire within you. And desire initiates the creation process within us. Remember that we are the creators of the universe; and the contrast that leads to desire is our raw material, our clay for sculpting.

You have a desire that is born from contrast, and there are only a few choices to make when confronted with this contrast:

- **You can condemn it and shout "NO," at it and start a war against it.** Which is what most of us have been doing from life to life to life. This does not reduce the contrast, nor does it fix what we are focusing on due to said contrast. Actually, it makes it bigger and brings it flooding back to us. The war on drugs has created more drugs. The war on terrorism has created more terrorism. The war on obesity has created more obesity. War begets war. Stop fighting everything and start focusing on what you want to accomplish.

- **You can rejoice in the contrast and be thankful that there is contrast to inspire desire within you.** When you see something or someone that is not pleasing to you, be thankful. Be thankful that that this thing or person is there to show you what you do not want, and to direct you to what you do. Be thoughtful toward that person in a positive and thankful way and then turn and focus your attention on what it is that you do desire and want.

- **You can simply ignore this contrast and go about your merry way.** This is the simplest and most morally objective way of living. If you do not like something and you do not put your focus upon it, and instead merely ignore it, you will not give it any more power to grow. Activists and politicians would have you focus solely on this thing you do not like, with pickets and boycotts and marches and rallies against it. This merely creates more of what you didn't want in the first place. So I say, ignore it; move on to something that is pleasing, and that you want more of. Then immerse yourself in it, rejoice in it and by doing so, create more and more of that which you do desire. If, however, the contrast keeps coming back to you despite all your efforts to ignore it, there is likely an important change needed. Go back to option 2 with this contrast and see where it takes you.

These are your three choices. I am sure with some debate we can come up with a thousand variations of these choices, but these are at the root. These are the boiled down, unpreserved, all natural choices that you have to choose from. Choose wisely and then hold to that choice, and the end result that you desire.

Remaining persistent and unwavering is really not as hard as it sounds. Though it will seem so in the beginning, just as any newly learned skill does, it gets easier the more you practice it. There will be tests and trials along the way. That is life. If you could step back and see your life truly from beginning to end, you would rejoice in each test and trial. For these experiences are the things that make life worth living.

As we have all heard throughout our lives, in once variation or another, nothing good or worth having comes easily. Anything that is worthwhile is worth working for; sound familiar? Well, let me put that concept into a little different perspective that will, hopefully, make it that much easier for you.

As I said before, it is not so much about convincing others as it is about convincing yourself. If you know yourself, and truly believe that what you are striving for is already yours, you are not going to stop until you realize this desire. Then what are all these tests and trials about if you already know it is yours? They are what you attract to convince yourself further and to strengthen your convictions. When you know that your desire is met and fulfilled, then you won't need tests and trials. We, as humans and creators, just like the challenge. We enjoy the work. If there are no tests for us to pass or fail and learn from, then what's the point?

Remaining unwavering is as simple and easy as remaining

faithful. This is the same faith one would give to God or to a parent when we were young. We knew that nothing bad would happen to us when our parents were with us. Just like the feeling that being in church, in God's house, is the safest place in the world to be.

Once you have come to know and love yourself as the GREAT, WONDERFUL, and POWERFUL being that you are, you will begin to have faith in your ability to create your life and your universe as you truly desire it. The more I learn about me and my true nature, the more in awe I become of what we as Humans truly are and can be. The power that we possess is truly mindboggling.

The greatest imaginations of our time have only just scratched the surface of the potential that lies within all of us. Superheroes and their super powers are more of a preview of what Humans are capable of than fantastic imaginary fairy tales.

Become your own biggest fan and really study yourself and the great potential that lies within you--within all of us. This will show you that the faith you need to be persistent and unwavering is as easy to obtain as seeing your reflection in the mirror. Truly know yourself and you will know God. We are all a part of that which we call God, Allah, Yahweh, Holy Spirit, etc. We are the physical manifestations of Source. We--you, me, and everyone--are Source energy, or God Force if you will, manifested in this lower vibration that we call the physical. When we die, we merely regain our higher more natural vibration and rejoin Source.

When you realize that we are everlasting Source energy, and that this life is not our "One Life to Live," life loses that manicness that has the whole world freaking out about everything. When you come to know that you are an extension of Source energy, you will realize that what is written in almost every religious and spiritual book is correct: we are all God-like because we are all like God. The potential within us all is only our belief, and a bunch of practice, away from fruition.

Know thyself and know God.

Healthy Self, Heal-Thy Self, Heal Thy Self! Healer, heal thy self!

By understanding your true nature, our true nature, it is much easier to be persistent and unwavering about our goals and desires. The realization that all is possible to you and for you by merely knowing that it is so, will catapult your life into whole new realms of possibility and excitement. The Universe at large is your play ground and your canvas; make something beautiful out of it.

Unwavering belief and persistence toward a goal has worked for every person who ever achieved a goal in their lives. Similarly, the majority of those people had absolutely no idea HOW they would achieve their goals, only that they WOULD achieve them. Steadfastness is the way to winning, earning, and achieving all that you want. Like the lesson in the fairy tale, The Tortoise and the Hare, if you stick to your path and always move towards your goal, you eventually will win the race.

STEP THREE: OPEN UP AND RECEIVE

Open up and receive!

Now that you are honest with yourself and know who you really are, you know what you want, and you know that it is yours, ***just because*** you know that it is yours. So what's next?

The Universe has one major law: the Law of Attraction. We are learning how this law works. First, we experience a contrast that creates a desire within us. This desire goes out into the Universe as a request. The Universe answers; in fact, it answers every time-- no exceptions, and the answer is always YES!

After all of that, you may be asking yourself, "Ok, if the Universe answers every time, why don't I see what I want?" Well, to be precise--if you have been honest with yourself and held persistently and unwaveringly to the outcome of what you have asked, then the only thing left to do is to accept and receive.

Sounds simple, doesn't it? Well, it is simple, but it's not easy. (always a catch, I know).

Step Three is really a combination of Steps One and Two, and is also singularly its own step. The idea here is that each step builds upon the previous ones. There is no exclusivity here from one step to the next. You cannot skip steps and go right to receiving. If you did, how would you know what you were getting from Santa?

Receiving is all about knowing, accepting and being. You know what you want. You know and accept that it is yours.

So, next is: knowing, then knowing and accepting, and lastly, knowing and accepting and receiving.

Like Lincoln Logs stacked neatly on top of one another, each step is necessary, essential and irreplaceable. The glorious thing about this process is this: by focusing on each step fully, you naturally are attracted to the next step; each step leads to the next, harmoniously and seamlessly.

By opening yourself up to the creative process of the Universal Law of Attraction, you can truly recreate your life, your world, and your universe.

Step Three: open up and receive. That's it. It is as easy as it sounds. Yet, many of you will mess up this part because you want to know where, what, when, why, and how. Don't be a reporter on your own life. By asking these questions and trying to figure out where things are going to come from, you are just telling the Universe that you do not have faith in the Law of Attraction or in your power of creation. And, believe me, I know how hard this seems. It is what has taken me the longest to learn and to master; and I'm still working on it.

My mind is always going; it is very analytical and scientific in nature: "A leads to B, which then leads to C," and so on. The problem with that is--and hear me out on this one--we are not even in the same ballpark of intelligence as Source (or God if you prefer). The Universe is a great and wonderful machine, here for us to use to create our bliss. All we have to do is have faith in the machine. Have faith in God, Source, All that Is, (or whatever doesn't make you cringe to say). What you call the

Universe doesn't matter to him/her/it in any way.

I'm not going to even try and entertain the idea that I might know more than God/Source/Universe/All That Is. I've got a REAL good connection to the other side. I know that and I am grateful for it. Where do you think I get all of this good information I'm putting on these pages? BUT, be that as it may, I don't have any grand illusions that I know it all, or what the future holds and neither do you.

Faith, my friend, it's all about faith. Once you give up the control, or more correctly the illusion of control, you will be astonished at how the Universe provides for you. From places you couldn't even imagine will come the fruits of your desires. The things you attract will come to you in the most harmonious way possible. The Universe will see to that. All you have to do is have faith in the Universe to deliver. Try to think of life as a wave that we are catching and riding. Your job is to get on and enjoy the ride, not to control the wave. Enjoy the ride!

We are great, wonderful and powerful beings; there is no doubt about that. However, we live in a linear time/space reality which gives us a limited view of our lives and the Universe. Conversely, the "Powers That Be" in the Universe do not suffer from this linear experience, and so can see the big picture-- from start to finish-- the whole story of our lives as we cannot. Therefore, we, as spatially challenged entities, need to trust in the Universe (or God, if you prefer) and the process. Trust in the process and the Universe to bring you what you desire and strive toward. The how is not your concern, and if you make it your concern, you are effectively throwing a monkey wrench into the whole works.

Faith and trust are very difficult things to learn for most of us. We do not trust easily and usually need vast amounts of proof to believe the most mundane of things. So, I would tell you to start with something small, something that you would be surprised to receive, but not break you if you don't. The lack of value or attachment to the outcome is a key element to this process. When something is yours, it is yours; there is no wondering one way or the other about it--it is just yours. This is the same way we must train ourselves to feel about the Law of Attraction and our creations. Therefore, the majority of the Masters out there today teaching about Deliberate Intent or the Law of Attraction will tell you to start small; not for the sake of the Universe, but for our sakes.

We start small so that we may ease our way into the creation process. Like any other skill we have, it takes practice, and the best way to practice is to start small and work your way up. This is true with all of the skills I've ever learned. You start small and manageable, and then incrementally work your way up; and before you know it, you are blowing the competition away. So, start small.

Start with something like a cup of tea, a certain book, or a phone call from an old friend you would like to talk to. Make each desire specific and unique to you, so that you will know that this thing has only come to you by using the creation process. There are many examples out there of how the Universal Law of Attraction works. Many of you may have seen or read *The Secret* or maybe some of the Abraham-Hicks materials, in which they give many examples of attracting small things to start with as a test or proof of the creation process. If you haven't seen any of these aforementioned materials, I highly recommend them. The more information you can receive, the better. This is a good rule of thumb when learning anything, but especially something as new and as different as this.

Make it your desire to find something, something specific and unique, and then see yourself holding this object, or being with this thing. Then imagine the scene in your mind as if it was a memory, as if it had already happened, and you are just remembering it. Do this and then release that desire to the Universe, having faith that the Universe is already providing this creation to you. Keep yourself in a place of unwavering and persistent faith, knowing that this desire is coming to you; and not only coming to you, but already yours.

Be open to those little nudges and hints that the Universe will put in your path to guide you--like bread crumbs--towards your desire. Within a period of time, determined only by how much of a match your vibration is with your desire, it will appear to you in a remarkable way that you never imagined. Then you will know, without a shadow of a doubt, that you created this. You used the Law of Attraction to create this thing in your world and now you are ready to move up to something a little bigger.

The main thing to focus on is feeling. Feel it; feel the feelings of it. By imagining it, you put yourself in a place that allows you to feel it. Feel the feelings of having it, the joy and excitement of that new thing or experience. If there is one thing that all avatars and teachers of this agree upon, it is this: we live in a feeling universe. If you want something, you must feel it. You must have the feelings of it. Feel it into existence.

How would you feel to have your new car? How would you feel to meet the love of your life? What would those things feel like?

Imagine them: pretend you have them; make-believe that you are receiving them right now, and feel how it feels. This is how the greatest manifestors in the world do it. They feel what they want into existence.

In addition, if you are busy imagining and feeling what it is you want, then you have a lot less time to wonder where it is coming from and when; and are therefore less likely to get in the way. Instead, you are more and more likely to receive all that you desire when you feel it into existence. Spend some time everyday imagining, pretending, and feeling the feelings of having and receiving the things you desire. Meditate on them. Quiet your mind and really get into that space of having and feeling. Be a child again. Pretend and imagine just as you did when you were a child. This is a wonderful way to get into that pure place of intention and manifestation.

Your life is yours to do with as you see fit. It's all up to you. Have fun with it. That is the real key to anything, have fun with it. This, and all things, should be fun. The secret to it is to do it for you. We are all unique and special beings on our own paths. We all have our own talents and strengths. Learn what your unique talents and strengths are and develop them.

Don't worry about anyone one else and what they have done. You are you and the idea is to do what makes you happy.

We have all come here for our own reasons and with our own paths in mind. Once you have accepted this and run with it, being the best you that you can be, you will have more fun and joy in your life than you could ever have imagined. All of these processes, and all of life, come into focus when you stop trying to be something other than who you are, and instead just be yourself. By being yourself on your own path, everything will feel joyful and wondrous. You will no longer struggle or fight. You will feel no need to struggle because you will be living as you were meant to; and everything about your life will make you happy and joyful.

"Follow your bliss!"

Joseph Campbell

WHO AND WHAT YOU REALLY ARE!
CHAPTER TWO

Who are you? What are you? Really, who are you? What are you truly? Are you your job? Are you your body? Is this life you are living who you really are? Are you more, or less?

I assume that most of you have asked these questions at some point. It is natural, for we are intelligent and curious beings. We are explorers and learners and creators; and yet, we are ever so much more than that.

This is going to be a chapter of great awakening for some of you; and for others, this may be the hardest to grasp. This is as it should be. You are all incredibly unique and special. No one answer I can give will answer all of your questions. However, by learning at least a little of who and what you truly are, you can begin to view your life in a much more beneficial way.

So, what are you?

You, we, me, all of us are eternal beings of energy. We

are everlasting energetic consciousness, living in worlds and dimensions of vibration, thought and creation. What is this energy that we are made of?

Energy, by definition is this: "Always was, always will be, and always is." It is in all things, is a part of all things, and is all things. It comes into form, through form, and out of form. It cannot be created or destroyed; it can only change form from one thing to another. We are all energy.

What is God? Ask a theologian and their answer will be something like this: God always was and always will be. God is in all things and is all things, and cannot be created or destroyed; and can take on and become any form desired. Sound familiar?

For you more scientifically minded folks, you only need to study a little about Quantum Physics to understand this. These statements have been proven scientifically, without a shadow of a doubt we can say that we are all energy. The most powerful electron microscopes have proven that all that we consider solid and "real" is merely a vibration of energy. Your body, your clothes, your car, and the chair you are sitting in; all of it is made up of the same stuff: Energy.

I won't go into too much detail about this simply because there is just too much out there on the subject, and many are far more qualified to discuss this topic than I. And since this book is intended to be entertaining and insightful, if I filled it with a lot of scientific evidence or proof of this, it would be neither of those things. So, I leave it up to you to do your own research on this incredibly interesting subject. As for me, "I have bigger fish to fry," so to speak, which is--we are all energy; and so, by definition we cannot die. We cannot be destroyed or created. We can only change form.

However, you may ask: what about death? Physical death as we know it is just a change of form. Who and what we really are will not experience death. We do not stop breathing and die' we go from physical form back to our natural state of spirit; or more correctly, back to our non-physical consciousness.

This is another subject that can be discussed forever. Not everyone will believe this, nor does everyone have to. Your truth is what you make it.

I like to think of our physical bodies as what they really are, a really advanced machine that houses our true selves for a period of time. We identify so much with our bodies though that it is difficult to think of them as other than who and what we are. There are other analogies and ways of thinking about our bodies.

I heard an analogy that I really enjoyed from an acquaintance of mine, Scott Christenson, a psychic medium and author of Bridging the Gap.. Scott said,

"Think of the ocean as the collective consciousness that we experience when we are out of body. When we are born it is much like scooping up your water/essence

into a bottle or your body. This separates you in your own little neat container so that you can experience the world or this life in your own unique way. This does not make you the bottle, but the bottle does become a part of you. Once your time is finished inside your bottle/body you are 'recycled' for lack of a better term and your water is poured back into the ocean. You are now back to your true and original self, your unique consciousness is once again a part of and among the 'IS' or greater consciousness. You are still you but you are connected to all that is. This is what it is like in our true form.

There are innumerable other analogies that fit and can be used as an example of our spiritual experience in this body and time space reality. Here is another that illustrates the point in a different way: when you go to the movies, you immerse yourself into that world and that reality, becoming one with the story. You laugh and cry with the characters, you feel for them and root for them. And then, the movie ends and you go back to your life as you know it. That experience of the movie does not change who you really are, but it may have given you a new lesson or something to think about.

I like to use this analogy a lot when I talk with friends about this subject. Simply because it fits so well, and also because all movies fall into two categories and no matter how you label them you can always break them down into those two main categories, which are Learning and Entertainment. Movies are basically for entertainment purposes, so that we can 'escape' for a time from our 'real' lives. You can also learn from movies. We all remember the 'moral of the story' at the end of some movies or television shows. Or maybe you like to watch documentaries to learn about far-off places that you may never physically visit in this lifetime. Either way, it's still a good time.

Life is much the same. If you break it down to its root purpose, it can also fall into the same categories of entertainment and learning. Hopefully, you are experiencing both of these separately, or in some cases at the same time. Life in the physical is the sum of the individual parts. There are many and varied parts, but if you break them all down to their root you will end up with the same things: entertainment and learning. We all have things to learn during our lives. Most of the time, we came into this body at this time for the very purpose of learning those things.

As for me, I've been wading through many lifetimes to get to this one, so that I can spread the word without being strung up, drawn and quartered, or burned at the stake. Because there are many more, like you, ready to hear what I have to say at this time than ever before. I am here to remind you of what you already know and only need to remember. You are all eternal pieces of God, The Source. We are not apart from God, but a part of God. We are the physical manifestation of God, Source,

All That Is; and we come to further develop ourselves on our spiritual paths, and help others, as well.

I sense that many of you have just asked "*THE* Question," and I will try to point you in the direction of the answer. The question, for those of you not aware that you asked it, is: "What is my path, spiritual or otherwise?

The best way, that I have found, to come to this answer is to go about it this way: You are an everlasting energetic being who has come to this physical time-space reality to learn something and to grow. Now, what is it? Well, start looking at yourself, your family, your personality and your passions. I believe, as do many others nowadays, that we are here on a pre-chosen path, a path of our choosing. We have all made choices before we entered this Earth and by looking at those choices and our traits, it will become much more obvious why we decided to come here at this time, and what we hope to accomplish.

Look at your parents. You chose them for a reason. What is that reason? What have you learned from them? How have you become the person you are because of them? Oh, and to give you a little hint: for the majority of us, our parents tend to teach us what we don't want, as opposed to what we do want. They tend to teach us out of negativity and fear, but do not despair, they mean well. Our parents, the ones who are in our lives, not the egg or sperm donors, only want the best for us and they do the best they can. They fear that we will not become what they hope we will. And, honestly, in most cases we won't. But, that is why we chose them to be our parents--to help us become who we intended to become all along, and to show us those things that would lead us to our desired results.

We are the sum of our parts and experiences. Start looking at those parts and experiences as if they had a purpose. You meant for them to have a purpose, and I bet you'll remember that purpose after just a little searching. Look at your personality and what you love. What is your passion? What would you love to do for the rest of your life even if you did it for free?

For me, I had my time of realization at the age of 29 when someone said to me, "You might be an Indigo; maybe you should write a book." For Alan, this was just a comment in passing, but for me, it started a firestorm of discovery and awakening. I will forever be grateful to him for this passing comment, even though I doubt he will remember me or ever having said what he did. This is how it starts for many of us; and that is how it started for me.

That comment started my research into Indigos, and into me. I began to realize my hidden potential and talents. I began by reading up on Indigos quite a bit, and analyzing what an Indigo was and how it related to me. I have since started to develop my talents and they have very quickly become my passions. I have received my certification as a Reiki Master since then, and have taken classes to develop my psychic abilities. In my classes we do clairvoyant readings and aura clearings and balancing. These are all wonderful things that I truly love to do. However, it has been my interaction with my clients and others within the class that have shown me my true passion and talents –and you're reading it. I am charged with writing works that explain such existential things as spirituality in a way that is understandable and palatable for anyone out there interested in learning about such formerly taboo subjects.

Luckily for me, I did not succumb to the pressures of the world to fall into line and become just another person following someone else's example while trying not to create waves. I found myself, and decided that, no matter what it cost me, I would be the best me that I could be. I want to teach and challenge as many people as I can, about who and what they really are, and what they are capable of being. I want you to realize this and do the same for yourself, and for the world. The more of us out there that are being ourselves and finding our own personal happiness, the more others will decide to do the same for themselves.

What we are as Human Beings are amazing and beautiful creators. We are GREAT, WONDEFUL, and POWERFUL spiritual beings living in a physical time/space reality to create, and to learn, and to grow. Do not hamper or hinder yourself from finding and loving the true and wondrous you. The more you know and love yourself, the more you are capable of knowing and loving others.

In the Bible, it is written that God and Heaven are within you. Do not search outwardly for something that is perceived as hidden, because you will never find it. You will not find it because you are searching in the wrong places, and asking the wrong questions. All answers and paths to God begin, and are contained within you. The spark that animates the skin suit, in which you live, is God and you. It is that which is truly you, and it is your pure connection to God. You do not need outside sources to find God. You do not need this book or anyone or anything else in order to find God. God is within. Find yourself by looking within, and you will find that which mankind has been searching for since the beginning of our modern age; you will find your connection to the Source that is the real you, and in doing so, find God.

"But, how do I look within?" You may yell in frustration because you've heard it before, and now you just heard it again. How does one look within?

"Know thyself." Who are you? What are you? Why are you here?

Begin by really learning who you are. If you followed the first chapter, then you are probably on your way to learning you. This is the one true path to any form of enlightenment. You must study you and learn all that you can about who and what you are.

Are you a builder? Are you a teacher? Are you an entertainer? Who are you really? What do you love to do? What are your passions?

I believe this is what is meant by the phrase, 'Soul searching.' By finding out who you really are and why you have come here, you will find your soul. You will find the real you. Once you have found out who and what you are -- and in the process find out why you came back to the physical -- you will know what you want out of this life. All things that you are curious about and searching for will begin to fall into place and your life will gain the meaning you have been seeking.

While you are looking at yourself and finding out who you are and why you're here, remember to be humble and honest. We did not all come here to be rich and famous. The majority of us came back to live very quiet and more meaningful lives, meaningful to us and our chosen path. Let other people be who they are and you be who you are. Finding true happiness in this life is about finding who you truly are and thereby following your own path.

If you are here to be a teacher, then teach. If you are here to be a healer, then heal. If you are here to be a good parent and raise wonderful children, then be a good parent. Whatever it is, why you have come back to the physical realm, own it and live it. If you are looking for the path to true and lasting happiness, it lies in walking your own path and not trying to walk someone else's. Be you, be the best you that you can be and know happiness and bliss. "Follow your bliss!", as Joseph Campbell said.

I cannot be you and you cannot be me. I cannot live for you, just as you cannot live for me. So, why try to be someone else or other than who you truly are?

I believe this is the biggest problem we face in the United States and all over the world, in modern first-world countries. Most are not happy, and almost all are searching to make themselves happy. Searching and searching, and yet growing more and more frustrated by the minute because they cannot seem to find what they are looking for. Everyone is striving to be someone else, or to have more and better things to find happiness, and yet after they change their faces and get more stuff, they are still not happy.

Why is that? Why is it that in one of the richest and most powerful countries in the world there is so much despair, so much unhappiness, so much longing for something to make us happy? Why is it that in a country that has everything in the world one could want, and everyone has the means to achieve whatever they want, do we find so much unrest and longing, so much depression and unhappiness? Why is it that an African country that does not have all the wealth and power that we possess in the United States ranks as the happiest country in the world, and yet we rank somewhere around the 26th happiest country in the world?

We feel without, because we are looking with-out of ourselves to find happiness. We feel longing because all of those material things and all that striving to be just like those people we admire on TV cannot bring us happiness. You cannot fill that void within you by buying more stuff, or pretending to be the newest flavor of the month star on TV.

The only way to true happiness is to just be you. Find out who you really are, and be the best and most wonderful you that you can be. There is no other way to find true and lasting happiness. There is no magic pill in a bottle and there is no amount of 'Stuff' that you can buy or obtain in your life that can make you truly happy and whole. Only by being the true you, and finding your path and reason for being here, can you truly obtain Heaven on Earth. God is within you; and by learning to be who you really are and have come here to be, will you reconnect with God, the Source, and with yourself.

However, don't take my word for it. Go out and do your own research into happiness. Go and explore this great and beautiful world for happiness and bliss. Go to Africa if you can, or to South America, or Tibet; or to any place in this world where the people seem to have nothing in the way of possessions, except a smile and a heart full of love. These are the places to truly learn what it really means to be happy and to find happiness.

In those places the people may have nothing (at least by our terms), and yet they are happy and joyful; and they enjoy life to its fullest more often than those you may be striving to be like. More often than not, it is these people who know the truth and the secret to being happy. They know that you need nothing in this world other than yourself and love to be happy. In many cases that is all some of those people have: themselves and love; and they know they have everything.

We have poisoned ourselves away from happiness in so much of the world in the past century because we see the 'Haves' and are killing ourselves to be just like them. And yet, we didn't even bother to find out if they are really happy, and if being them is really all that great. Nope, we just thought:"They have all that stuff, it must be great to have all that stuff, and so they must be the happiest people in the world because they have all that stuff!"

But are they really? When you read the newspapers, or watch the news on television, do you see those people as happy? Sure, some of them do seem happy; yet not that many stay that way, do they? Why is that? What is it that makes those people--that so many are striving to emulate--unhappy?

There is an emptiness felt in this country, and all over the world, that comes from within. We've tried to fill it with so many other outer things, and it is still empty and painful. And, that is the problem! We've tried and tried and tried and failed each and every time to fill that gaping hole inside ourselves with so much stuff. It is now time to learn from our mistakes, and try something new that will fill us up and make us whole and happy.

> *"Do you know the definition of Insanity? It is doing the same thing over and over again, and expecting a different result."*
>
> **- Albert Einstein**

It is time for all of us to move past this desperate striving we've lived in for so long, and grab hold of what it is that will truly make us happy, which is Ourselves. 'Know thyself and the world is yours!'

Stop trying to be someone else! Stop trying to compete with the Joneses! Stop trying to find happiness in something you buy at the store! Stop all of this nonsense and get simple!

You are you! You cannot be someone else other than you! You cannot, and should not, try to be someone other than who you really are! You must realize that being 'You,' and being the best 'You' that you can be, is the only way to true happiness. Period. The End. Leave the package by the door, Th-th—th-th-That's All Folks!!

You are the most wonderful, powerful, greatest you in the world. Learn who you really are and appreciate all the wondrousness that is you.

Now, let's just stop for a minute and take some time to ponder this. Who are you?

You are human. You are living in the beginning of the 21st century on the planet Earth. In these ways you are very similar to the rest of us. But, that is obvious and meaningless. What I am concerned with, and what you need to concern yourself with, are all the wondrous differences that make you, you.

This world is a wonderful symbiotic place. Everything and everyone has a purpose here and is a part of the greater whole. Where do you fit in? What is your part to play?

You may ask, "Who me? What is my purpose?" I am a writer, a teacher, and a healer. I am here to help you to remember things you may have forgotten, and/or to challenge you in one way or another to think in a new or different way. That is my purpose, and the part I am here to play. I want to let you know personally that I truly appreciate you for giving me the opportunity to be me by you reading these words on these pages. If you were not you, and you didn't have a thirst for knowledge, then I would not have someone to be me for.

That is the symbiosis that I am talking about. Stop and think for a minute about all those people in your life that you pass by and interact with every day. Believe it or not, you serve a purpose for them and with them; just as they serve a purpose for you and with you. No matter how small or seemingly insignificant you may think that purpose is or the meaning behind it, know that it is as much a part of the greater whole as any other part. The smallest piece can cause the greatest damage by being removed at a critical joint or juncture. Do not belittle the significance of small things in your life or others. Remember, it is the little things that matter most.

Start looking at the little things that make you who you are. Look at your likes and dislikes, your talents, and just as importantly, the things you aren't so good at. These are all little pieces that make up the real you. These are the things that make you perfect for someone else and make them perfect for you. No one is perfect, they say, but maybe you are perfect for them and they are perfect for you. How will you ever know who and what is perfect for you if you are busy trying to be someone or something other than yourself? You cannot and should not try, because it probably won't end very well.

Find those people in or around your life that you haven't noticed or paid attention to yet, the ones who are always smiling and happy. Especially the ones that do the same things, day in and day out, and never have a negative word to say. These people carry great wisdom about life and being happy no matter what. Strike up a conversation and make a new friend. You'll be wonderfully surprised at what you can and will learn by talking to those you probably felt sorry for in the past.

Mainly, and most importantly, they will tell you and I will tell you now: **'KEEP IT SIMPLE STUPID!!'** We make so much out of every little thing when it isn't at all helpful. I am going to spend more time later on with this subject, but I felt it was necessary to mention it here, since it is also relevant to this topic and so many others.

Now, back to you --learning you, and being the best you that you can be. Have you started to look at yourself in a different way than ever before? I expect you have, at least a little. This, like all other new skills is, and will be, a work in progress. The more you practice, the better you get. Start with small steps, and stay focused on completing each step before going to the next. Before you know it, you'll look up and realize you've climbed the mountain. You knew the result you wanted, and you focused on the steps while holding to that outcome, and here you are. You have begun to see yourself as the wondrous person you are, who is perfect in your imperfections and finds happiness by just being yourself with others that appreciate you for you.

I know this is a lot to take in and to try to absorb and implement, but I know you can do it. You have the power within you to change your life and the lives of those around you, just by being you. I want you to take a moment to breathe and relax. Take a deep breath and let this information soak in for a bit. While you are breathing and relaxing, I want you to think about all the 'Cool' people you've ever known in your life from grade school until now. Oh, and I mean the really cool people, not those that tried to be cool by being mean to everyone because their Daddy had money and they wore nice clothes. I am talking about the truly cool people, the original people who didn't have to try and be cool for anyone, they were just cool. What is the one thing all of those people had in common? What made them cooler than the rest? They didn't care what others said about them; they just were who they were, and made no apologies for it or took any crap for it.

It is those individuals who make the largest impact in the world, because they don't spend their time trying to be anything or anyone but themselves. This frees them up to accomplish great and wonderful things, because they do not waste energy trying to be something other than who they truly are. Think about all the energy and time we've all wasted in the past trying to look like, act like, fit in with, or be someone else. Staggering isn't it?

I want you to know that I am able to write these words because I am not immune to the stumbling blocks I've listed. I went through all of this. I wanted to be someone else. I wanted a different name and a cool exterior. I wanted so much to be those people I admired and looked up to. Yet, it wasn't until I stopped trying to be someone else and just started being me, that I began to feel like I wanted to feel and gained the attention I so longed for. When I began to be me and didn't care what anyone thought or said about me, I found what I had been looking for all along.

You do not need to be anything other than the great, wonderful, and powerful person you were born to be, that you chose to be, to find all the happiness you deserve and are rightfully entitled to. God, the source of all things, is a part of you and within you. God does not think you need to be any more than what you are. God knows you are perfect and expects nothing of you. Just be yourself and honor the piece of

God that is within you and that is the 'Real You.'

Follow your heart, your mind, and your emotions to open up Heaven on Earth. The greatest gift anyone can give themselves is the permission to be who they really are. Be true to who you are and those things you love to do, and you will find bliss without measure. You were not meant to come to Earth and suffer. You were meant to come here and live happily, while creating a wonderful world of joy and bliss. God did not tell you to suffer. God does not want his/her children to suffer--no parent does.

I know that many of you may have just had the next logically skeptical thought that sometimes comes after reading the last few paragraphs. "What about pain?" I'll take a little bit here to address the subject of pain and hopefully put it into a better context for us all.

Pain is a reality of the physical world in which we live, yet it should not be the norm; rather, it should be the exception to the rule. Pain is a tool for learning. It is the greatest teacher we have ever and will ever experience. We must begin to look at pain as the great teacher it is. We must begin to appreciate pain and the lessons it teaches. The lessons are not pleasant and are not meant to be. What would we learn if we didn't experience pain occasionally? Do not fear pain. Respect pain as the teacher and learn from it. The more you learn from and appreciate pain for the lessons you receive, the fewer lessons and the less pain you'll need.

Pain is not as painful when you can realize the lesson behind it. Pain is not as scarring when you can see the good behind the lessons it teaches. As I have said, pain is our greatest teacher and our most necessary teacher, because we live in a physical time-space reality. We live in bodies of flesh and bone that can break down if we are not careful. This means nothing to our true selves as spirit, but it would be a shame to come all the way down here and go through all of that because we wanted to accomplish something and learn something, only to break this vessel before we were meant to and have to do it all over again. So, we endure pain to teach us how to survive in the physical and keep this wondrous machine we call a body as long as we can, so we can learn and experience as much as we can.

I am going to spend a lot more time explaining, in later chapters, the spiritual reality of our true selves, and what we have come to do in our physical bodies in this time-space reality. I am trying to keep all of this information flowing and understandable, and although it may get off track a bit here and there, all of the information is related. It isn't always possible to consistently stay rooted in one subject. I apologize for this, and ask that you take your time and keep on reading. I promise you that the light at the end of the tunnel is growing brighter, and it will all start to make more and more sense the further you go.

Now, to recap what we have learned thus far: know who we really are; how to find happiness by truly being ourselves, and the purpose and meaning behind pain. Where shall we go from here? Let's find out, shall we? Turn the page and let's continue our journey together.

NOTHING IS BAD AND BAD IS NOTHING!

CHAPTER THREE

Just as the title to this chapter states, "nothing is bad". You may be wondering how I can make such a statement. How can I make such a claim if I live in the same world you do, with all of the horrors and atrocities that occur on a daily basis?

To put it simply, I can because I look at things in a different way. As you may recall from the previous chapters, I explained that the only thing we have true power to control in this world is our reaction to it. If you do not want to experience the horrors of this world, turn away from them. Jesus said to "turn the other cheek," and I believe this is what he meant. You do not need to experience all the horrors of this world unless you choose. You choose to by watching the news or scanning the Internet. The effects of these "bad" things all over the world cannot affect your life unless you let them.

Now, don't get me wrong; I am not saying this means you should be uncaring and callous towards the rest of the world--quite the opposite, actually. We need to focus our considerable energies on all the good in the world so that we can create more of it. As I stated before, yelling "No" at something, or fighting against something, does not make it go away; it only makes it stronger because we put our energies into it and feed it.

Start by appreciating the good in the world. Appreciate others as your fellow human beings who deserve all the love and happiness that you do. Look at all the random acts of kindness and all the happiness and laughter in the world, and focus on that. That seems a far better use for your valuable energies than focusing on all those things that upset and distress you.

Do not resist the negativity in the world. Just like you know not to react or give your attention to a small child who is acting out, or to a bully who wishes to demean you, so it is with this, because you know that the more you resist, the more they persist. The same can be said for focusing your attention on those negative things that you wish to change. The more you focus on them, the more they persist. For example: the "War on Drugs" has only created more drugs; the war on terrorism has created more terrorism, and the war on obesity has created more obesity. Declaring war on something or fighting something only makes it grow and gives it more strength.

I rarely if ever quote the Bible, but in some cases; such as this, 'The Good Book' does come in handy. There is a passage in the Bible that quotes Jesus as saying; "Resist ye not evil", which is basically saying the same thing, just in a translated 2000 year old dialect.

As we are rediscovering, our attention and focus has more

to do with what happens in our lives than any other thing. We know how often we focus negatively on something and how often we tend to get our wish about that thing. We know now that a simple shift in our thought processes can shift our whole life and outlook.

Try this little experiment: The next time you are out driving and someone cuts you off, or cuts in front of you a little too close for your liking, instead of lashing out at them and throwing fingers at them or cursing them, try saying, "You're welcome;" or "Come on in." Mean it as if it were a friend of yours who just made it to join you in line at a movie or a show. Embrace that person as a friend and allow them in as an act of brotherly/sisterly love and kindness. Say things like: "Oh, just made it;" or, "Wow, good job getting here." You will be astonished and amazed at how this minor shift in your reaction will make you feel.

By not allowing that negativity to flare up and lash out, you do not allow it to compound itself with the other person's energy and then reverse back on you, making you feel awful. You turn it into a game, like playing tag as a kid. How many times did you feel exhilarated and joyous when whoever was "IT" narrowly missed you and you got away once again? These are the feelings you can have while you drive, instead of feeling anxious and angry about "all those bad drivers out there." Oh and by the way, we all think we are good drivers and drive better than the next person; but like anything else in our world, that's as relative as everyone else's opinion.

Now let's review the last two paragraphs and look at what

changed: the only thing that changed in that situation was how you reacted to it. It was the same situation in every detail except for your emotional reaction and outcome. What was this big and mysterious secret that suddenly changed your world? Your reactions are the best, easiest, fastest, and only real way to change your life for the better, today and forever.

One of my favorite examples of this is the old truism, "Two men looked out from prison bars. One saw mud and the other saw stars." Another is the story of two toddlers at the beach with their mothers. Both were sitting at the edge of the water, giggling as the little waves tickled their toes. A bigger wave came and washed over the two toddlers. One screamed, ran to his mother and clung to her leg for dear life, terrified of the water. The other squealed in delight and turned to face the ocean to await the next wave. The exact same thing happened to both the toddlers in the same way at the same time and place, but their reactions to the event were not only polar opposites, but set their lives on very different paths.

Once you have practiced this for a time--and, yes, it does take practice like everything else--you will start to see how easily and wonderfully this simple shift can make your life seem: magical, blessed and wonderful.

For you more linear-minded people out there, here are the nuts and bolts of what I am saying: What you are doing is retraining yourself to a state of non-reaction, or to a positive reaction, to those things we previously trained ourselves to react to in a negative fashion. When something happens that upsets you, do not react negatively but take a deep breath and smile.

Look at whoever is causing this distress for you as you would a child of your own who is just acting out for attention or out of frustration. Do not react as you previously would, but react as a loving parent with infinite patience. Allow these things to happen and/or merely avoid them as best you can.

The strongest oak will be snapped in a strong enough wind, but the willow will just bend in that wind and then retake its former shape once it stops blowing. Be flexible and allow these things to roll off you like the water off a duck's back. Standing firm and being rigid only makes you easier to break. Being flexible and flowing makes you strong and resilient, harder to break.

My favorite way of affecting quick change in my life, and allowing myself to allow others to have their 'moments' (without causing me any undue hardship) is to take a 'Big Picture' attitude. Here is what I mean by that. When you run into those things that irritate you, take a moment to look at the big picture of your life. In the big scheme of things, how is this minor incident going to affect the rest of your life? The answer, of course, is as much as you let it.

Is making that next light worth betting your life? Is winning an argument worth your relationships or family? Is not letting the guy in who is trying to merge in front of you worth it in the end? The answer to all of these questions is obviously "No," or at least it is for me – now that I've practiced this for a while.

Take some time to think of occasions when you wasted a lot of your energy over something that was meaningless. All those angry honks and gestures on the road, or red-faced screaming matches through glass or an open window at sixty miles per hour don't change anything. And it doesn't matter what either of you say, because neither can hear the other anyway.

It just isn't worth your valuable time and energy.

Begin to value yourself more than that. Value your time and your energy the same way you value your money. Appreciate yourselves more, and don't waste any more of your time and energy on fruitless pursuits. Once you value your time and energy and stop wasting it, you'll have more and more for those things that are really important in your life.

We must learn that what another person thinks or says doesn't matter, and cannot affect us unless we let it. Remaining calm and peaceful in the face of adversity is in and of itself its own reward. How nice is it to let others have their "moments" and not be affected by them, but just let them occur in a state of non-judgment. We all have our "moments" as human beings living in this physical world, so why not rejoice in and appreciate these "moments" as a needed release that is soon to pass.

Hanging onto and continually repeating a scene in your mind is like beating a drum or banging your head against a wall; it's doing something, but it doesn't really get us anywhere. If you experience something that you did not like, do not dwell on it, but replay it once in your mind--the way you would have preferred that it have gone-- and then let it go. Never dwell on anything you do not desire, because that only creates persistence in that thing and keeps you from creating the things you do desire.

Oh, and try to keep those replays positive in nature. Don't replay a violent victory in your head, even if you really want to. Negativity and violence, even if merely thought about, begets more negativity and violence. The Universe does not distinguish between what we perceive as "actually" happening from what happens in our minds, because our minds can't tell the difference either.

Here is an example of what I mean: Many of the US Olympic teams have adopted a training program of running their events only in their minds as a part of their practice regimen. When these athletes where hooked up to machines that monitored their brains and bodies during these imagined events, their muscles fired in the same sequences they would if they were actually running the event. This shows that the mind does not distinguish between what we consider real from what we imagine. Therefore, since our mind is our most powerful tool, and the mind cannot distinguish between the "real" or "imagined," imagine away. Imagine your world the way you want it to be in every detail, and keep doing so to begin to turn your life around for the better--from the inside out.

"We Live Life Inside Out!" Now that is a good way of looking at life. All change and all action begin within each of us. Every movement begins with a thought. Every sound begins with a thought. Everything we have known or experienced began as a thought. Stop and ponder that point for a moment. Everything began as a thought: The Universe, the Earth, the animals, the people—all began as a thought.

Quantum physics has proven that there is no life without mind coming into it. You cannot look at an atomic experiment under an electron microscope without influencing the outcome. Similarly, you cannot live in this world without influencing your life and everything around you with your thoughts.

Your thoughts can be measured. They have a wavelength. Use them wisely.

"Bad is Nothing!"

Here is the point of what I want to say in this chapter. Your world is what you make it. The point of view you choose to adopt can and will affect everything in your life. By adopting the "woe is me" attitude you will only create more opportunities for you to experience a "woe is me" life. Conversely, adopting an attitude of a friendly Universe here to do your bidding can only bring to your experience that very thing. How wonderful is that? How awesome is that opportunity for you? What will you create with the power of the Universe?

There is nothing occurring in this world, this plane of existence, that can harm you or cause you pain, unless you let it. There is nothing that is "bad." The point of view you adopt determines how you will perceive this world and all that occurs in it. What is simply is. Judging something as 'good' or 'bad' can only come from your limited perception.

When you begin to perceive this world as a place of experience and learning, a place for eternal spiritual beings, living within biomechanical suits, to further create within and grow the universe and their spiritual selves, you will begin to see that nothing being experienced today can harm you because the real you is eternal and cannot be harmed. You may have chosen to live in a less than desirable place on this Earth for that very experience. You may have chosen to align yourself with many less than positive occurrences within this lifetime to learn from and use them to potentially break a cycle or pattern that you have spiritually outgrown.

Here is an example of what I mean: Think of a video game. How many millions of us have immersed ourselves within a video game for hours on end? In many of these games you are working towards a specific goal. In the pursuit of said goal you may have died fifty different times trying to "make it." Did the dying of you on screen deter you from completing your mission? This is very similar to what it is like for our true spiritual selves when we choose to experience these "physical" lives. We have a goal, lesson, or experience in mind that we wish to accomplish, and we will not stop until we have completed our goal. Most of the time, it will take us several lives and bodies to accomplish this goal, just like in the video game.

I realize that many of you may be saying; "But, that's totally different because it is just a game and that person on screen isn't real. I can't be hurt if that fictitious video game character dies or is dismembered, but I can be hurt and die if I did those things in "real life."

I ask that you bear with me for just a moment and consider this: You as an eternal spiritual being cannot die and cannot be harmed by anything that occurs to your body. If the body dies, the spirit lives on. The real and true you lives on no matter what happens to your body, or how many bodies you go through.

Now I ask you to think back to when you played those video games (or if you prefer the movies you've watched). How many times did you put your character into positions of great danger and death for the fun of it? How many movies have you watched that portrayed killing and maiming throughout the movie so that you would feel the thrill of fear, if only for a moment? Why is that? Why did you want the experience? Granted, it was through a fictional third party, but you still wanted some part of the experience.

This is no different than what your true spiritual self is doing with each of your "physical" lifetimes. We want experiences. We want to learn and grow; and the best way to do that is through our experiences. As we all know, we learn best from our experiences and especially from our so-called "negative" experiences.

I realize that this may be a hard concept to grasp for many of you. That is very understandable due to our limited physical time-space reality viewpoint. We have a very difficult time looking at our lives in this bigger picture context, because of this limited view. All I ask is that you try it. Try looking at your life from more of a third party view point. Look at all of your experiences as an outside observer. Just try to look at the things in your life that had an impact on you and remove the emotional attachment you have to it. Remove the feeling of it, and look at the before and after you. Look at your life in a more clinical or scientific way. Look at the cause and effect of the things you have experienced as if you were looking at someone else's life, and see what you have learned and how you have changed and grown.

The more you practice this, and the more you use this process of re-evaluation, the easier it will get; and the more your perspective toward your life will grow and change. This process is the best way to move away from all the simple and small things in our lives that drive us crazy. This re-evaluation process helps to change the way you react to those experiences in your life that you formerly considered negative.

Just looking at your life as just one long learning experience that never ends (because you never end) will take a lot of the stress out of it. By knowing that you are an eternal being who cannot die and does not end, but merely changes form from time to time, you can begin to relax more and more about your life and begin to really enjoy the experiences of it. This is what we are really here to do anyway.

Every experience is positive in some way, shape, or form. Look for that positivity. Grab those lessons from each experience and rejoice in them. Life is about the journey, not the destination. It is about the experience, and not the end result.

Year by year, month by month, day by day, and minute by minute, your life is about experiences; and each experience you have creates what you call your life. Your life is, after all, just the sum of your experiences.

Why not begin to enjoy them? Even the ones that may not be so pleasant at the time can be enjoyed by learning from them and seeing that learning as positive.

It may seem like a monumental task, but like all journeys in life, it begins with a single step. Take the first step. You will be astonished at where you end up by merely taking one step after another.

Now, I would like to delve a little deeper into this train of thought and give an example of what I mean. This may strike a chord with many of you in one way or another.

Let's look at someone who experienced a horrific experience at a young age as an example. There have been many such events recently – terrible earthquakes, tsunamis, and mudslides that wiped out whole towns, killing and maiming all inhabitants. These unfortunate experiences affected people's lives dramatically. Due to these events, people have gone through a lot of emotional upheaval and pain. Given some time and space, some will make use of therapy and counseling, others will pick up from where they are and move on with the knowledge of what they have, and therefore can, survive. Some will grow, out of their experience, into strong and self- assured people. They will become who they now are because of those events in their past. Does the end justify the means? Does who they are now and what they learned from that experience change it from a negative to a positive? The experience itself will always be seen as a negative, but embracing the change it caused will change the focus from negative to positive. That being said, not everyone will choose to grow from their experience. Some will crumble into helplessness, hopelessness, or anger. And, it is their choice to make.

Let's look at this scenario from a spiritual journey stand

point? Is it possible that they chose to have that experience to create a change within them or to spur them into action to create change? What if they wanted to break out of a cycle that had spanned many lifetimes with their current soul group? By going through that experience and creating that desire for change they were able to break that cycle and get away from those people/souls and start a new chapter, a new journey. This was only made possible because of those events in their life.

I have a friend who was horribly abused by her own father for many years beginning as a toddler. A while ago it was popular to talk about Serial Ritual Abuse or Satanic Ritual Abuse, SRA. My friend experienced it in all its horror, her first violation occurring at 18 months of age when her father raped her. That was the least of her horrors because the cult enjoyed terrorizing the children by locking them in dark boxes with bugs and other creepy crawlies. The children were sex slaves to anyone in the cult who wanted them. When "God" was mentioned, they would bring out large dogs and inform the children that God spelled backwards is dog and then force them to have sex with the dogs. They would be taken to the rituals and be forced to watch all manner of vile behavior before they were made to take part. What positive could come of such terrible experience? That's what my friend asked for many years. She considered herself a shattered and damaged human being.

What a difference a slight change of perspective can make. After beginning to associate with a group of loving and enlightened women, she began to realize that skills gained through the horror were valued and valuable. She eventually accepted that she had indeed chosen her life and that the only way to gain the knowledge and skills she sought was through the life she had led. She realized that her father may have been her best friend, agreeing to play the role of monster to help her reach her goal. Today she is successful in her career as well as able to use some of the things she learned for the good of others. While she does not look back fondly, she is happy with what and who she is and will be as a result of all she has experienced.

I realize the example(s) given may be hard to look at for some of you. But the point I'm trying to make is that no matter what happens in your life, you have the power to turn that negative into a positive, and rejoice in what was once a source of pain, because it became a catalyst for you to grow. Look back on all those things you went through that you once viewed at as negative, and know that these events made you stronger, happier, and wiser. Life is all about the experiences and what you get from them.

The best way for this to affect change in your life is to make sure you are always moving through your experiences. Move through them and learn from them. Too many times people have become stuck in an experience. Instead of moving through it and learning from it, they are continually reliving it in their current life and cannot move past it. They are stuck in a sort of purgatory--forced to relive that experience over and over again. Little do they know that with a little help and a shift in their perspective about that event, they can transform it from the most defining negative event in their life to the most defining positive event of their life. Many of the strongest and happiest people in the world have experienced some of the worst atrocities we have ever heard of, because it was those experiences that made them so strong and happy. They have been through the worst, and it changed their perspective on life.

These are the things we must do as a people. Change our perspectives on the experiences in our lives and grow from them. The growing from an experience changes it from a negative to a positive when we realize what we learned and how we grew. **"That, which doesn't kill us, makes us stronger."**

Those of you that have been, or are in the military can understand this very easily. Just think about basic training. For most it is a means to an end. It is not a very enjoyable experience at the time, but by knowing the outcome and persevering through it all, those that do are changed in a positive way. They feel stronger, more accomplished, more self-assured and more confident. We can adopt this same sort of thought process to our everyday lives and change how we look at our experiences.

By shifting your consciousness and thought processes towards a more positive mindset, a bigger picture mindset, you can turn any negative into a positive. When you are going through a rough patch when money is tight or you are sick, just remember that this, too, will pass--and you will be stronger because of the experience. We as humans living in this physical time-space reality will have our ups and downs, but we don't have to suffer because of them. Being positive and rejoicing in those moments when you really just want to give in and be depressed and negative, will make a world of difference for you. Doing so will make those times pass faster and will give you the greatest sense of accomplishment -- having weathered the storm with a smile on your face and a song in your heart.

To suffer is a singularly human experience. Animals do not suffer. If left to their own devices all animals live joyful lives no matter where they fall on the food chain. They do not fear death and do not mind being eaten. It is only through human interaction with them that they feel suffering; usually due to the fact that when we feel it, animals then feel it from us. When you are miserable, doesn't your cat or dog want to come and be with you to try and make you feel better? How do they know? They know because they feel it.

Be more like an animal and be more natural. Stop concerning yourself with so much nonsense and just live life in joy. Find joy in everything you do. And, if you cannot find joy in something, then do something else: make a change.

I find that by simplifying everything as much as possible, this process is much easier. All the stuff we pile on day after day makes it very difficult to look at something objectively and find the joy in it. ***"Keep it simple stupid!"***

YOU CHOSE THIS LIFE!

CHAPTER FOUR

Let's look at a concept that is probably new to most of you: You chose this life to live. You chose this life before you were born. You chose your parents. You chose to be born into that family, at that time and to those parents, for a reason.

WHY?

Why would you choose this life? Why would you choose these particular parents? Why, if you could choose any parents in the world, would you choose these?

I am sure many of you may have responded by saying, "Because I didn't choose them!" Are you sure? Let's look at you and your life, assuming that you did choose to be born to those parents and into that family. Why would you do that?

Let's look at you parents to start with. What kind of people are they? Were they both there? Were they good, bad, or indifferent? What did you learn from them? What did they teach you? What lessons came from them that you are now trying to work through?

Here is how I look at it. You can decide for yourself if it makes any sense to you.

I chose my parents because the lessons I wanted to learn and the things I wanted to work on during this lifetime would best be suited to them. I wanted a mother who has a very similar mindset as I, not only to raise me but to become a friend and partner in teaching and helping others. I wanted my father to teach me about how to be and not to be a man, control issues, forgiveness, and to be my own person no matter what, even if that doesn't fit within his own criteria of acceptance.

By looking at your parents as the two halves that make up who you are, you are able to discern what you wanted your purpose to be. In my family's case, my mother and I are quite like-minded, while my father is very grounded in his own world of experience and does not easily accept new concepts. Now that I know that, how do I take from it my life's purpose?

By looking at the two halves that make up who you are--and figuring out how you would bring them together--you can get a good idea of who, and what, you are. For example, I am here to try and take these things that I know and put them into a format that will be palatable to the everyday guy who may have very little, if any, experience with such things. How do you tell someone who is very intelligent about the world we live in, with a myriad of other topics in his head, who has raised you, and will always see you as that small boy needing guidance, about things he has rarely, if ever heard of--like intentions, energy, spiritual plans, and how thoughts are the most powerful force in the Universe?

Look at your parents and their differences and similarities. Look at whether they were there for you or not. Look at what the word "Parent" means to you. These are the things that will enable you to begin answering those lifelong questions of: "Why am I here?" "What is this life about?" "What is my purpose and plan for this life?" and so on.

We as a society love to pass the buck and not take any responsibility for ourselves. "It's not my fault! It's my parents fault, they raised me." Don't be so sure about that. What if you chose them to raise you? Whose fault is it then? The fault and the answers many times come together within the same person.

The answers that we are searching for are always within us--within you--within everyone. It is a matter of being brave enough to start asking those questions and looking for the answers.

There is plenty of help out there to find those answers from others who want to help you, whether they are willing to help themselves or not. So, don't despair; there is help if you want it. You don't really need it, but it is there.

All it really takes is a willingness to be brutally honest with yourself and to look at your life as a detached observer. Look at all those things that make you who you are. If you chose this life to do and learn something, what is it?

Maybe you chose this life not to do or learn anything. Maybe this is a vacation life and all you want is a very simple life, with a very simple outlook. Perhaps you chose this life to be an entertainer, so that you could entertain the world. Maybe you chose this life to be a doctor, or a healer of some sort, so that you could help your fellow humans. Maybe you chose this life to do nothing more than experience it, by wandering the Earth as a traveler. There are countless possibilities and variations, but at the root, there is still only the one question to answer: Why did you choose this life?

Here is another thing I like to think about from time to time, which helps me to put this physical time/space reality existence into perspective. What about the old saying, "Only the good die young"? What does that mean to you? For me, it points out that this life isn't our natural state. If the good always die young, then that means to me if you're good, you get to go home sooner, and if you're vile, you get to live on this plane for a very long time. Or maybe the lessons we need to learn, and how quickly we learn them, determines how long we stay on this plane. Or possibly all those extraordinary young people come into this life knowing they won't be here long; and are here for the sole purpose of inspiring others and touching their lives in some way. Once their job is done, they go home.

Every life has meaning and is purposeful; none are wasted or in vain. As a great and powerful eternal spiritual being that cannot die, each of these excursions into this realm of existence has meaning and purpose. However, because we are everlasting eternal beings, you don't have to feel pressured to do or be anything that you do not want to be. You are everlasting, as is your spiritual experience and journey; therefore, you will never finish it, and therefore can never get it wrong or mess it up. You have infinite lives to live, to learn, to grow, and to experience. Take a little of that pressure off yourself. You do not have to get it all done this time. Oh, and in case you were wondering, that old adage about having only one life to live is wrong. We may only know of each life as we live it; but that only serves to keep us focused on this life and what we wish to accomplish. We are all eternal pieces of the great I AM. We have lived, and will live, many more lifetimes than we can dream of.

How does this work for you now? How can you use this information to help yourself --now? Well, as with all things, that is up to you. Here are a few of the positives I have found in my life by using this thought process: I value each person in my life more now, be they family, friends, or acquaintances. I look to each person and to that relationship as a lesson. I ask myself, what have I learned from them or what can or will I learn from them and the relationship?

Some of the hardest experiences and memories from my past have lost their sting and stigma now that I look at them in a positive way; by viewing them as lessons I needed to learn in order to become who and what I am today.

This is one of the main themes of this book and of my life: You are the sum of your experiences and knowledge. By revisiting old wounds in a different mindset you can take away the pain that you held onto from that event and turn it into a positive.

Let's revisit an example I gave in the previous chapter about being in the military and experiencing boot camp or basic training. This is necessary for anyone who joins the military, and generally is not one of the most pleasant experiences in one's life. However, if you ask anyone who has served about the hard training they went through, most of them would not trade it for the world. That training changed them and made them who they are now. Granted, most of us would not choose to go through it again, but we all value having been through it.

One way to look at those hard times in your life is to realize that it is all training for the future. Life is like that. Until we as a human race can figure out a better way to learn things, the hardest lessons in life will still be the best.

We have explored how your mentality and perception can change your life; Here is another example. Take responsibility for your life **as if** you chose to live it. Take time to prove to yourself that you knew what you were doing and that your life is "on purpose," . . . or don't!

You see, that's the beauty of being human: free will. You can choose to do, or not to do, whatever you want. The power lies with you, and only with you. Ask anyone who has ever been to rehab or had an intervention--if they weren't ready to take responsibility for themselves and help themselves, no amount of "help" from other people would change that.

You have to do it for you, and only you can do it. You may ask for help, and you may get the help you ask for, but the responsibility will always lie only with you.

What an awesome realization it is when you finally understand that you are in control, and it is solely up to you. Some may find this a bit stressing and worrisome to suddenly realize that they are the ones in charge of their lives. But I tell you it is the most wonderful thing in the world to know you are the master of your life, and it's only about what you want to make of it. Go big, or don't. You have the controls and can do anything your little heart desires with this life of yours. Oh, and if this is a bit too much for you right now, don't worry; you can always come back and try again.

You chose this life! You truly did. And once you can accept that, and realize the potential you possess from the choice you made to be here now, you will be in awe of yourself.

Life is wonderful and was meant to be so. Take the time to own your life, and make it as wonderful as you desire it to be. Or, if you prefer, you have the right to make it as miserable and as awful as you can imagine it to be. The choice is yours, as it has always been, and always will be.

I would also like to commend and congratulate all of my soul brothers and sisters out there for choosing to be here now. This is a most amazing time to be a spiritual being having a physical experience. We are nearing the end of the Piscean Age and heading into the Aquarian Age. All of the doom and gloom predictions of the end of the world and 2012 are merely mistranslations or propaganda set up to scare us into blind obedience by Church and Government.

When you research these topics and go far beyond the religious dogma, going back to the original astrological meaning of it all, you will realize that what is being taught and feared is just a bad mistranslation being manipulated to keep us all scared and impotent. The "End of the World" described in the Bible that so many are focused on, is a mistranslation, or more likely a cunningly placed bit of propaganda.

In the Bible, when we are told about Jesus talking about the End of the World, what he is really saying is the end of the Aeon (Eon), which means Age. The Earth and our entire galaxy are in a cycle, or cyclical procession, through our Universe. Just like the Earth revolves around the sun along with the other planets, our solar system revolves around our galaxy and our galaxy revolves around the center of our Universe. Every 25,765 years we pass through all 12 Ages (named for the 12 signs of the Zodiac) and that completes one Great Year. Each Age is approximately 2150 years, and as previously mentioned, corresponds with one of the 12 signs of the Zodiac. For the last 2010 years, give or take, we have been living in the Piscean Age, or age of the fish. Around the year 2000, we began the last 150 years of this Age and are moving into the new Age of Aquarius, or "The Water Bearer." As stated in the Bible by Jesus, the end of this Age will be marked by a man bearing water, and we should follow him into his house, knowing that the symbol for Aquarius is a man pouring water from a pitcher; and each age is considered to in the house of whatever symbol it falls under.

At the time of Jesus' birth, we were passing from the Age of

Aries, the Ram into the Age of Pisces, which is symbolized by the two fish. Which, coincidently, is the symbol for Jesus; and we see this symbol of the fish throughout Christian mythology. Jesus is represented by the fish: Jesus befriended two fishermen, and he fed 5000 people with five loaves of bread and two fish, and the list goes on. And, if you still need proof of this, just keep your eyes open the next time you are driving your car: the Jesus fish is displayed prominently on the back of millions of cars.

The reason this time is so great a time to be alive is due to this transition into the next age, and not the so-called "End of the World". Many illusions and lies that have been perpetrated on all of humanity will be exposed; and many will begin to see through the veil of lies. This shift in consciousness will begin an age of awakening and awareness for all of humankind. The "powers that be"--church and government--will be exposed and ousted from power. At least, that is what I hope for and foresee. Otherwise, we may as well place collars around our necks and accept our fate as the slaves we are.

We have been lied to since before recorded history. These lies and illusions that we have been living under are being exposed for what they truly are--a means of control over the masses by the few. Now is the time to wake up before it is too late and we all end up living in a one-world government controlled by the banking cartels and power brokers. It is said that "Power corrupts and absolute power corrupts absolutely." Take a look around and see if this is not the case today. Those that have the money and the power have been consistently moving toward the sole goal of world domination and control.

The theme of world domination and control has been romanticized by the media and popular culture as a far fetched myth portrayed by the evil antagonists of the Bond films and many more. The best lies contain an element of truth. This is exactly what the richest families in the world have been striving towards for thousands of years. Every war, conflict, recession, stock market crash, and depression can be traced back to the world banking regimes as acts of control and profitability. All these things have been orchestrated to steal our power from us and lull us into a false sense of terror so that they can steal more and more of our freedoms and enslave us.

Yet, even after saying all of that to you, you still have the choice to do as you will. Empowering isn't it? Your awareness creates your reality and the world you experience; use it wisely. Continue to expect and visualize the best future you can imagine.

Far too many of our fellow humans, possibly even yourself, are slowly losing their minds and their health due to unnecessary stress, caused by worrying about and trying to fight against the very things I've mentioned above that we find wrong in the world. Just remember this little tidbit of information the next time you feel your blood pressure rising and that little vein in your neck and head starts to pulse: "What we resist must persist." And, "Where your attention goes, energy flows."

What you 'Pay' attention to,
You have just Purchased.

Do not fight against anything you want to stop--that will only empower it. Change your focus to what you do want, instead of those things you do not want. To change the world, you much start in the mirror and with yourself. Change your thinking and your own world, and become an example for others to aspire toward. Focus on all the positive that you want to grow in the world, and let others see and hear you doing this. Be as unwavering and persistent as a loving parent would be with a child having a fit. Hold to the outcome of your desire and don't let the naysayers discourage you. Use all of your incredible power with love and joy. Be open, accepting, and understanding of others' fear and ignorance--of themselves and of their own power.

Embrace yourself as you truly are: the Great, Powerful, and Mighty Spiritual Being with Dignity, Direction and Purpose. Truly love yourself as the rest of the Universe loves you. Acknowledge your power and presence and become the ray of loving sunlight that you are--that God sent here to bless the world as a reflection of him/herself. Get to know the real you and love yourself gently, as gently as you would a newborn baby.

LISTEN TO YOU!

CHAPTER FIVE

Now then, how are you feeling so far? Still with me? Still want to continue with our journey through the exploration of you and your perspective? I sure hope so, because we are getting to the really good stuff now.

However, that being said, this may be a good time to take a break and absorb some of what you have read so far. If you are a fast reader, then just take a few minutes, or an hour or so, take a walk, or just sit and meditate on what you have read. If you are like me and take a little longer reading, you could take a day off, or even a week to process this information. However, don't go too far for too long. Life often happens when you aren't looking and you may get swept away. Stay close enough to remember to pick this book up again and continue with our little journey of spiritual self exploration.

OR.......

Do whatever you feel like doing. Remember, I am just a guide and bringer of information. You are the one looking for answers on your quest for truth. You must listen to you and go at your own pace. You are the unique and perfect expression of Source in the physical, and only you know what is best for you.

Now, that being said, the first step is to be completely and brutally honest with yourself about who, what, and where you currently are. Do not let all those little nagging fears, pictures, and illusions you have been living with all your life sneak up behind you and pull the wool over your eyes again. Be persistent and unwavering on this journey. Take just one step at a time, and take as long as each step takes, but do not stop moving forward.

As James Arthur Ray says (and I love this by the way), "Balance is not perfection, balance is stagnation." When you look at a scale that is balanced, what is actually occurring? NOTHING! The two opposing forces are canceling each other out. Balance is stagnant, balance is death. In this world of our physical time/space reality, one of two things is happening, either growth or death. In the natural world, things are either growing or dying. Plants never cease to grow until they die, just like we never cease to learn and grow until we die. Or, more correctly, we come into a body to continue on our spiritual journey of growth and creation; every 80 years or so we take a breather to check our progress and decide what to do, and which way to go, next.

What you want to find is harmony, just like an orchestra coming together to create beautiful music. Each individual piece on its own sounds odd, incomplete and may sound out of tune, but once you put them all together they form a wondrous musical experience. That is harmony; and that is what we as spiritual beings having a physical experience are really needing and searching for. Do not balance yourself into stagnation and death. Harmonize with the rest of the world and let that beautiful music play.

In doing this, you must first find your instrument, your chair, your music and your director or composer. This is where the fun, and the real work, begins.

Let's look at you: Who are you? What are you? Why are you here? What is the purpose that you have found for yourself? What is your passion and what are you doing with it?

Now stop looking around to your spouse or parents, or whoever it is you look to when someone starts asking you these probing questions. No one knows you better than you do. Stop living by the opinions and expectations of someone else and start living by your own expectations and opinions.

Misery comes from realizing you are on the wrong path, but being too afraid to do anything about it. Look around you at all those people you see everyday that are angry at the world because they are angry at themselves for settling. Never, ever, ever, ever settle for anything less than your worth.

And, once again, in case you are wondering, as a Great, Powerful, and Mighty piece of the Great 'I Am,' with Dignity, Direction and Purpose, you are worth as much as the Source from which you come. The only limitations placed on you are those placed by you. Your own lack of belief and faith in yourself is what holds you in a place of not having. As I said before, only you can do it for you; do not listen to others' opinions when it comes to you--especially if those opinions are in contradiction to who--and what--you truly are.

Listen to you! Period. The end!

Some of you may be thinking that this is not the best idea in the world. You may be thinking that if everyone only listened to themselves and only did what they wanted, the world would turn to anarchy and chaos.

Well, to that I say, have no fear my friends. Truly selfish self awareness merely means that everyone will do exactly what we are meant to do and will be exceptionally happy and content doing it. This would effectively end all conflicts in the world, because it is very hard to get upset and fight about anything when you are happy and joyful.

There are billions of people on this little planet and there are infinite possibilities for each and every one of us. Size is nothing to the Universe and in case you hadn't heard, the Universe is expanding. As we continue to live in this physical reality and continue to create our worlds, we continue to add to the expansiveness of the great Universe in which we reside as a little speck of sand on a cosmic beach.

Stop limiting yourself and your thinking. The great faith talked about in all the world's religions is misdirected toward a faraway and invisible God. Direct that faith towards yourself and your great potential; and in doing so, you truly will glorify God by fully realizing the power and potential that God placed within you. Do not doubt, do not fear; you are an everlasting spiritual being that cannot die. And, if you happen to break this body in the process of your journey, don't worry; you can have another one, as many as you need, as a matter of fact.

True courage lies in not limiting yourself to save the feelings of others, which is what we are really doing. We live in a perpetual state of mediocrity because others are afraid to see us succeed as it may make them look bad. This is not your problem--it is theirs. You cannot limit yourself due to others' fears. This only lessens the greatness of all, and of the Source that placed you here to fully experience your power and greatness.

"Our deepest fear is not that we are inadequate. Our deepest fear is that we are powerful beyond measure. It is our light, not our darkness that most frightens us. We ask ourselves, "Who am I to be brilliant, gorgeous, talented, fabulous?" Actually, who are you not to be? You are a child of God. Your playing small does not serve the world. There is nothing enlightened about shrinking so that other people won't feel insecure around you. We are all meant to shine, as children do. We were born to make manifest the glory of God that is within us. It's not just in some of us; it's in everyone. And as

we let our own light shine, we unconsciously give other people permission to do the same. As we are liberated from our own fear, our presence automatically liberates others."

- Marianne Williamson

Do not expect others to graciously allow you to grow and shine. As you begin to truly explore your power, others will do everything in their power to hold you in mediocrity. Do not allow anyone or anything to discourage you and to stop your forward momentum. As we learned in Physics, the law of Inertia states; "A body in motion tends to remain in motion until acted upon by an outside force; a body at rest tends to remain at rest until acted upon by an outside force." Therefore, it is hardest to start something moving that is still. But once in motion it becomes harder and harder to stop the forward progress as it picks up momentum. Do not let another person stop you before you start and do not allow them to slow you down once you get started. Hold fast and strong to your path and progress; and before you know it, you will be blowing past them all. And suddenly, when they realize they cannot stop you, they will begin to idolize and emulate you. Be an example of power and strength for the rest of us; let your light shine as a beacon to all others to do the same.

Show your true power and voice and encourage others to find theirs. This is the true path to greatness and harmony. Become the light in your own life that you have been seeking, and thereby show others their own light.

Jesus, the Buddha, the Dalai Lama, and all great Avatars and Masters have said the same thing: "These things and more that I have done, will you do also." They did not wish to become the messiahs and the gurus for the world, but rather serve as examples of our own innate potential. Study the great books and scriptures and you will see that this is the truth; it is written there for you to find.

By being yourself and honing who you truly are to a fine razor's edge, you effectively become an instrument for the greatest good. As we all have observed from our lives, those things that we concerned ourselves with in high school quickly lost their importance as we grew and matured. Those that were ridiculed due to their individuality and so-called oddity during those years, are many times the ones we come to admire and envy in later years. Those were the ones that had the courage to be themselves, no matter the consequences or disapproval from others. They were not to be pitied, but admired and hailed.

This simple lesson, to which we can all relate, still rings true for most of us. Those daring enough to move forward as themselves, despite what others may think, are the ones who create a more beautiful world and provide examples for the rest of us to follow.

I suspect that even now the voices have started in your head about why you can't do this. Why "They" (whoever they are) won't let you; or why it isn't practical or possible right now.

If this is what you're thinking, it isn't you. You would not hold yourself back from the true greatness that is within you. However, others would; and those are the voices in your head. Maybe, it is the voice of a parent. Out of love for you, he didn't want you to be disappointed. So he embedded in you the thought that you can't or shouldn't do what you desire. Or, perhaps it is the voice of society at large, who out of fear of their own failures being magnified by your success; want you to swim the waters of mediocrity. Misery and mediocrity love company, my friends-- yet daring and bravery need only you to come forth.

I do not proclaim to know everything that is happening in your life, or how hard you perceive your life to be. I only say this: You want change. You feel it in your bones and you know that whatever your life is now, you deserve more and better. How do I know this? First, you're a human being living on the planet in this three dimensional time-space reality. Second, I know that you are a perfect reflection of Source, striving to realize your true power and potential. Last but not least, if you didn't want more and better for yourself, you wouldn't have picked up this book and spent your valuable time reading these words.

It is vital to release all of those nay saying voices in your head and begin to listen to you. Ignore all the voices of mediocrity and begin to think greatness. What do you have to lose? Those voices and opinions will always be there for you to come back to if you so desire. Besides, how well have they served you so far? It's time to start thinking outside the sterile boxes in which we find ourselves. All great inventors, thinkers, teachers,

Avatars, and businessmen think outside the box of mediocrity and normalcy. If they didn't, they'd be just like everyone else who daily grinds out a living in misery.

Life is meant to be joyful and abundant, not mundane drudgery. Our world today is a construct of the few (who know they are) powerful, wishing to stay in power by easing the rest of us into complacency. Whether "The Church" or political puppet masters, they do not want you to think for yourself and realize your true power and potential. They would like you to continue to buy what they sell you, eat what they tell you, live the way they tell you, and, most of all, continue to fill their pockets, and give away our power.

As quoted in a previous chapter, "Power corrupts and absolute power corrupts absolutely." This quote describes a reality in which most of us live every day. We have willingly given up our true power because we think, "That's just the way it is; this is the world and these are the rules." Yet, if that is the case, why are we wanting for more? Why do we feel denied? Why do we feel like we are missing something, and that "This can't be IT; this can't be the way it really is." If this is it, why are we here? What is the point of life if we accept as reality what we are shown and taught every day? Is it only this mundane drudgery that has us all imprisoned and miserable?

The power "they" are talking about is not really power, but a scam. It is a system designed to keep us ignorant of the truth of our own power. True power, the power that we all possess as pieces of Source--as pieces of God--is freeing and liberating. True power comes from within, when you stop listening to "them," and start listening to You. True power comes from knowing who and what you truly are, and running with it. Do not resign yourself to mundane mediocrity because "everyone else is." You are not everyone. You are you; the one and only perfect piece of God, in the flesh, here and now.

Take a moment to stop and think about what you've just read. Take a moment to think about how often you have allowed yourself to be held back because of someone else's opinions, fears, and mistrust. How many hundreds and thousands of times have you allowed yourself to be an accomplice to your own mediocrity, in which you now reside and desperately wish to escape?

Notice that I used the term, "allowed". As I have said many times throughout this book: You are Great and Powerful Spiritual Beings with Dignity, Direction, and Purpose, living in a physical body to experience life in joy and abundance, as God intended. The only reason you are not living in that way, is because you have allowed others to talk you, teach you, and pressure you, into giving up your power. We have no one to blame but ourselves for the situations we find ourselves in, myself included.

No one can make you do anything you do not wish to do! Period! What are they going to do? Kill you? Big deal! You are eternal beings and death is nothing more than waking up from a physical dream you were having.

I realize that may be a little melodramatic, but it is nonetheless true. You must own your power as a human being and no longer allow others to dictate to you what your life is and how it is going to be. The greatest of the great that we admire, idolize, worship and emulate, did not stand idly by and let the masses dictate to them who they were, or what they were going to be. They stood up as Great and Powerful beings and declared who they were and what they were going to do. That is true greatness, and it lies within each and every person on this planet, in this galaxy, and throughout the Universe.

Now, before I get some of you too riled up and causing a ruckus all over town, let me say this: Owning your power does not mean throwing it in others' faces. Owning your personal power is that quiet confidence that comes from knowing who and what you truly are. You do not need to scream it from the rooftops. Just be yourself and do not allow anyone to change your mind about who you are.

As an example of this, you can look at monks, gurus and masters of many philosophies or teachings to see what I mean. They are accepting of all others and unyielding about themselves. They have such a firm grasp on who and what they are, that there is no need to confront others or try to convince them; they just are.

This is really one of the greatest lessons I ever learned, and I hope this is also a large part of what you take from these pages.

I am who I am, and you are who you are. We are both pieces of the same Source. We are made up of the same stuff. We are Human. We are Spirit. We are one and the same, and yet wholly different and wonderful. I acknowledge the greatness within you, and all of those who inhabit this world; and in so doing, I also acknowledge the greatness within me. I respect others as I respect myself. I try to acknowledge all those that cross my path with a simple head nod and a smile. I am merely saying hello to my fellow human, my fellow spiritual warrior in the flesh, and to myself.

Once you begin to see yourself as made up of the same stuff, as pieces of the same Source as everyone else, you begin to realize that to demean or to cause harm to another is really demeaning and harming yourself. By accepting and loving others as much as you can, you are accepting and loving yourself.

The Golden Rule, as we all know, states: "Do unto others as you would have them do unto you." I'd like to rephrase that a little to make it even more powerful: "Do unto others as you would do unto yourself, because you are."

Dannion Brinkley often talks about his death and near-death experiences. One thing he said that really made me sit up and take notice about how I treat others, and therefore how I treat myself, was his description of the Panoramic Life Review that we all experience when we "die." We've all heard someone say, "I saw my life flash before my eyes." That is a reference to the Panoramic Life review.

Dannion describes it this way: When you leave your body and are once again back wholly in spirit, you have this Panoramic Life Review in which you get to relive every moment of your life in startling detail, so that you can judge for yourself what you accomplished and learned. When you are done reliving your life from your point of view (or reference if you will), you get to become every person you ever encountered and experience the interaction from their point of view. You actually feel how they felt, how your interactions affected them. In effect, you get to be every person you ran into in this life, and get to feel the effects you had on them.

Man! If that's not incentive enough to be a little nicer, I don't know what is.

Stop and think now about just a few of those encounters with others that you may not be all that proud of. Now imagine that you are that other person and you get to experience that event as them. Yikes! I know there are a few I'm not looking forward to reliving when I head home. But, I'll tell you this, I'm sure going to try and make as many of my future encounters as pleasant as I possibly can. You can bet your pretty pattooty on that!

So, what am I saying with all of this?

When you stop listening to others' opinions, knowing they are not you and are not living your life for you, and instead start listening to yourself as a Great and Powerful Spiritual Being with Dignity, Direction, and Purpose--then you will begin to know your true self. And knowing your true self, you can then begin to act on those things that matter to you, and that make you who you really are. You can stop ALLOWING others to side track you on your path, and start building up your own life and power momentum. Then you will truly and happily begin to enjoy your life as the wonderful learning, growing, and loving experience it is meant to be.

Oh--and here is another point I want to make in this chapter--food for thought, if you will. I may have mentioned this earlier, but I think now is an excellent time to revisit it.

I want you to answer this question in your head before reading the next line: "Do we all live in the same world?"

What was your answer? If you said, "Yes," you are wrong; the correct answer is "No." Why do I say this?

Think about the subtitle of this book. We all live in a different, little, private world of our own creation, because of our singular perspective. We purposefully remove ourselves from the spiritual consciousness, and separate ourselves within these bodies so that we may have a singular experience to create as we see fit--to learn and grow on our spiritual journey.

No two people living on this planet will ever have the same life experience. No two people will ever experience the exact same things. And, even if they do happen to be in the same place at the same time, experiencing the same event, neither one will experience it the same way, due to their own personal perspective.

Stop and think about you and your friends, your family or co-workers, or anyone else you interact with regularly. How many times has something happened that greatly affected the other person, but had little or no effect on you, or vice-versa? Your perspectives, mentality and experiences are different; thus you both reacted differently. This is why we all live in separate worlds of experience, or reality, if you will.

I hope it will be a little easier for you now to go out and be yourself, while enjoying and allowing others to be themselves. Oh, and if you're not laughing, you're not doing it right. Spirit is joyous, and so are you, if you're on the right track. God, the Source, the Great Is, is joyous and full of love; and as part of All That Is, joy and love is our very essence.

Be yourself, know yourself, and above all else, love yourself! Because if you don't, who else really will?

HAPPINESS COMES FROM WITHIN!

CHAPTER SIX

So, we know that our mentality creates our reality. We know who and what we really are. We know that nothing is bad and bad is nothing. We know that we chose this life to live, and that we need to listen to ourselves first and foremost. Now what?

As you can see from the title of this chapter, I want to discuss the subject of happiness now--the true happiness that we are all longing and striving for in this life; the kind that is obtainable, and not some "Holy Grail" to be quested after and never obtained. All you need is a little awakening and a shifting of your perspective.

All of your life depends upon your perspective, your point of view. Happiness is no different. Why is it that in the United States, one of the richest and most affluent countries in the world, we rank about 26th on the happiness scale, and a third world African nation ranks 1st? How can this be?

It's all about perspective. We have been trained and

brainwashed into wanting more and more and more. We think the next little trinket or goal will make us happy, or "Once I achieve my degree, I'll be happy, "or "When I get that new car I'll be happy," or "Once I get married and start a family, I'll be happy," or "When I earn my first million I'll be happy," and on and on it goes, with no end in sight.

Trying to keep up with the Joneses (or the Rockefellers, if you prefer), is no more than an unending treadmill that gets us no closer to true happiness than the next trinket we buy. Once again, my friends, we are running after other people's ideas and ideals. We are a world ruled by the media and advertisers rather than by our own best interests and common sense.

It is so ingrained in us today that we don't see any problem wiring up everyone to the World Wide Web through computers, PDAs, Blackberries and cell phones so that we can all stay connected. Stay connected to what? The propaganda mills that are telling all of us what to eat, what to drink, what to wear, and what will make us happy?

It is insanity, people, and it needs to stop. We need to open our eyes and ears and see what is really going on. We are puppets on the strings of the great advertising gods and masters of marketing and media. We have lost the ability to think for ourselves and to decide what is best for us on our own. We now must turn on the news, or grab a paper, or get online to find out what is best for us and what we "should" be doing. The more "connected" we become to this Media brainwashing the less connected we are to our true selves.

I am not saying we should all move out to Tibet or Outer Mongolia and hide from it all. I am merely saying it is time we get back to the ones that really matter and start listening to them first: Ourselves! As we covered in the last chapter, you must listen to You, first and foremost. You are the only one living your life and the only one who knows what is best for your life and for You.

It is nice to acquire things, and new shiny things are always great, at first. But, then the wanting starts again almost before it ended with your last purchase. It's always more, more, more; and the more you get, the less happy you feel--so you go out and get more to make you feel happy. But it never works. Like an addict who is looking for the feeling of that first high over and over again, but never achieves it.

Why is that? Why is it, that the more we obtain, and the more we buy, the less happy we truly feel? I believe it is because we know deep down inside that it is all a lie, and a superficial cover-up to disguise our enslavement to someone and something other than ourselves. We have become imprisoned in this material world of marketing and the "Next Best Thing". We are consumed by it and enveloped in it. Even those that rebel against it, and declare they are against the "Evil Marketing Machines," get caught up in their own little version that tells them what type of hybrid car, bicycle, sandal, or all natural vegetarian food to eat.

Let us not get caught up in what is "evil" and who is pulling the strings, because it doesn't matter. It is what it is. We chose it and now we can choose something else. We listened to these messages and we bought into the hype and propaganda. Granted, this onslaught started almost from the moment we came into our new physical body, but it seems that at some point in all of our lives, there was a moment when we realized we were missing something, or that there was something off about our lives. How many of us made that conscious decision to find out what was missing and tried to fix it? How many put up the good fight for awhile but then succumbed to the overwhelming pressure of, "That's just the way it is" thinking?

Don't get down on yourself, or be too hard or critical on you. It's not a problem at all. You can live your life as you see fit and you will never get it wrong; you will never come to the end. Our spiritual evolution is all about timing and being ready for the next step or leap forward. And, many times we find ourselves taking several steps backwards before that next leap forward; but that is only so our spirit can get a running start to make the next leap. Embrace your life and all its steps and phases. Know that each and every step or misstep becomes a necessary part of our growing process, of our evolution. Rejoice in all the mistakes and errors, because these are our best teachers. If it were not for the pains and pitfalls we wouldn't have learned a better way.

Now back to the subject at hand: happiness. Happiness comes from within. How many times have we heard this and how cliché does it sound to you now? It is similar to the concept, "We are all one," that we have heard so many times, and yet have a hard time believing; yet it still rings true. Happiness comes from within! It must; because all creation and all things begin within each and every one of us. A single thought or feeling, just like the pebble into the pond, starts the ripples outwards that can influence the entire world.

All invention, all creation, everything started out as a thought from within. Why should happiness be any different?

Look back on what you have read, and what we have covered so far. What is the common thread? What is the theme of this entire book? Answer: You and your perspective. You are the master of your universe and the creator of your world. Who else can provide you with happiness? No amount of stuff you see on television or on the internet can give you what you seek. You must find it for yourself, and you must start your search with the person staring back at you from the mirror.

All of the greatest avatars, masters, teachers, gurus, messiahs, and just plain people throughout our history, have said the same thing about you: The power to change the world lies within you. However, we have all thought this meant the power to change the entire world or planet resided within us; and while that power does reside within you, you must begin with you and your world first. No one person has ever changed the rest of the world for the better, before they first changed their own world for the better.

You must start with that one thought and feeling, and then grab on to it and let it ripple out to the rest of your life. Find that happiness within yourself, and let it ripple outwards towards the rest of your life and self. The journey of a thousand miles begins with just one step and so goes the journey of your life.

We must all stop looking outward for happiness. It is a futile pursuit that will lead to nothing more than want and despair. All of the problems of our lives can be managed once you find that peace is within yourself.

When you peel away the layers that have been piled on and wrapped around you from years and years of other people's thoughts and opinions, you will begin to get back to the base and root of you. The deeper you go, the calmer and more centered you will feel; until you come to that place of inner knowing and finally know that you are the source of your own happiness.

I don't want to mislead you in any way. This is not simply a matter of sitting down and closing your eyes for 30 minutes and "presto," you suddenly know your inner self and you are happy. We are humans, and as humans that would be too easy. We can accept nothing worthwhile without having to fight for it. I'm sorry to tell you, but that's just how we roll.

It took you years upon years, and lifetimes upon lifetimes to get you to where you are today, and you will have to dig yourself out from under all those layers to get back to the true you. You may have to relive many unpleasant things from your past to understand them anew as something necessary and ultimately positive to who you are today. You must peel away each and every layer that is covering up that primal and pure you underneath.

For most of us, this may take several lifetimes or decades or years. For those who don't like to take the long road, there are places to go to speed up this process; but like most things they come with a price, and is far more unpleasant than taking the time to ease through these layers. But, like ripping off a Band-Aid, or jumping straight into cold water, it is over more quickly. Just remember, please, that there is no hurry; there is no rush, no reason to quit your job, or leave your family to search for your own enlightened master so that He or She can beat you back into a semblance of your true self. That would be a bit extreme and completely unnecessary; plus it denies you the greatest joy of all: the Journey.

Life, including all the lives we have lived, and will live, are about the journey and the experiences. Do not deny yourself that joy of experience and of the journey. I merely suggest taking a step back as often as possible as you go on your journey of self towards happiness, and remember to acknowledge the journey and to look back on where you were and how far you have come. Trudging forward with your head down will get you there, but you will miss some great views along the way.

True happiness comes from each and every moment in your life. It comes from each breath, each step, each drink, each meal, each song, each laugh, and each and every minute, of each and every hour, of each and every day. When you are aware, each and every moment of each and every day, of who you truly are and of your journey as spirit in body, then you have found true happiness. Not from the acquisition of things, but from the experiences of your everyday life as You.

We all, myself included, tend to get too caught up in our next thing, our newest project, or our next goal and we forget to enjoy the fruits of our labor from our last accomplishment. We race blindly forward and miss all of the beauty along the way. People, we've got to "stop and smell the roses," and not only stop to smell them, but to appreciate them from root to tip; drinking in every detail, with all of our senses and fully experiencing the beauty of the rose.

You may be saying, "But, I don't have time to stop during my busy day! I've got to go, go, GO!" Why? Why must you go, go, go, and deny yourself the greatest and simplest pleasures of all? The simplest and greatest thing you can do for yourself, and the world, is to slow down and just enjoy being you right now. Stop and look around, take a deep breath, and feel you being you. Totally and simply, you being you, in this body, now.

Need an example of how you can be you in the moment? Just look at your pets or someone else's pets, or maybe watch a documentary of wild animals lying around in the sun. I watch my cat as often as possible when she doesn't know I'm watching her, so that I can see what it looks like to just be, enjoying the moment and therefore truly enjoying life.

Animals don't have any problem at all with happiness and the enjoyment of life. They are just happy to be alive and experiencing being alive. We can all learn a lot from the animal world. We may have forgotten that over the millennia, but animals can and will show us many of the secrets of life, if we simply open ourselves up to them and learn.

You do not need anything else in this world to make yourself happy, just you being you is all you need to find happiness.

Too often we begin to associate our own happiness with the company of others. Too often when we are alone with ourselves we go stir crazy and start calling everyone in our phone book to come and rescue us from ourselves.

STOP IT, PEOPLE!!

Quiet time alone to just be you being you, is a priority to a healthy life and healthy living. Just for 30 minutes or an hour, stop being Mom or Dad, Boss or Kid, Student or whoever else you may be, and just be you being you in the moment. Breathe in life and love you, just because you are you, on your journey through life and experience.

Too often we lose ourselves in what we consider our responsibilities, and soon enough we don't know where we end and the other person begins. We may ask, "Who am I really?" "Am I just Mom or Dad?" "Am I just a Doctor or a Lawyer?" "Am I just a struggling house wife with two kids and no husband to help?"

No, my friends, you are not just those things. That may be a part of your life now and a part of who you are now, but it is only the smallest part of who you truly are. Come back to your roots. Come back to the base of you and reconnect with You.

Have I gotten off track? Have I lost you along the way? Did you think I was going to just say, "Hey happiness lies within, so look within!" Sorry if I have disappointed you, but it's never that simple, is it? It will take work on your part to come back to you, just as it took work for you to get away from and forget who you are. All those steps away must be walked back. But, have no fear, there are short cuts and you can run, skip, and jump, all the way back to you. It is totally and completely up to you, your personality, and your perspective, which way you choose to begin your journey back to the real you. As long as you begin the journey, the rest will work out fine.

Happiness lies within you **and in no other place.** You may find it in other people, places and things, but it won't last for long unless you are already happy within yourself. Then each person, place and thing will only multiply your happiness and joy. This is what I wish for myself, for all of you, and for the entire Universe: True Happiness and Bliss.

SIMPLICITY IS BLISS!
CHAPTER SEVEN

Now then, let's get cracking at some more common sense answers to our everyday problems. "What Problems?" You may ask. Well, the keeping up with the Joneses, for starters.

As I've mentioned before, we as a society are ruled by the media, advertisers and fear-mongering news companies. All day long, we hear, "Buy this and you'll be happy," or, "Don't go outside, there is a killer on the loose," or "Join the Home Shopping Network and fill your home with knick-knacks you don't need."

We have become an empty society, trying to fill our emptiness with stuff. We buy newer and better stuff in an attempt to make us feel better about ourselves. "Look at what I just got! It's the latest thing," we shout from the rooftops. Then, once the newness is gone and everyone else has the same newest and latest gadget, it's time to start searching for the next new thing to fill that ever-expanding void within ourselves.

However, the more you buy, and the more you obtain, the bigger that emptiness gets, not smaller. It is a self-feeding, self-fulfilling prophecy of greed and excess. The more you get, the more you want. And, before you know it, all those things that you believe you own, start owning you.

The United States of America has become so brainwashed into believing that the accumulation of things is the quest of our lives, that we hoard things "just in case." Did you know that this is something we find extremely common here in the States, but is almost unheard of in the rest of the world?

That's right. Storage units are a uniquely American invention. Only here do we need a place to put all the stuff that won't fit in our current home so that we can save it for later. Yet all the while we are accumulating more stuff, so we have to get bigger and bigger storage units to hold all of the additional stuff that we aren't using. And to top it off, we pay rent on the storage units that hold all of this extra stuff we aren't using. So, even though you believe you own it, you are still paying for it.

It's amazing when you step back and take a look at it. We do not fill our lives with the joy of experiences anymore; instead, we fill our lives with stuff--stuff that weighs us down and makes it harder and harder to move on to newer, bigger and better things--and all because we have to drag all this stuff along with us. It's really sad to see someone who wishes to move to the city of their dreams in order to fulfill their own personal desires, yet all that they have acquired over the years prevents them from moving, because the cost of living is higher in the new city and therefore they can't afford a house big enough to hold it all.

Like an anchor holding a ship in port, your belongings tie you down and hold you back. You are held back from the freedom of movement and desire.

What would you have to do now, in your present state, to grab a bag and run off to Europe for the summer? Sounds like a great idea doesn't it? Backpacking across Europe, staying in hostels, making new friends, and seeing the beauty of all those countries; so, why don't you go?

Like many of us, you may say, "Oh, I can't just pick up and go. What about my house? What about my job? What about all the stuff that I would have to leave behind? What would happen to all my stuff?"

This is a very common theme for us: "I'd like to do X, Y and Z, but I can't because of A, B and C."

How much freer would you feel if you did just drop everything and run away to experience and live life like a rogue traveler? What adventures would you have? How alive would it make you feel? What responsibilities do you believe you have that makes a dream like that seem impossible?

I am not suggesting that everyone quit their jobs, sell all their stuff and leave their families behind to run off on an adventure. And, even if I did suggest it probably only one-tenth of one percent of you would actually go through with it. Besides, that sort of thing isn't for everyone and the majority of you over the age of 25 wouldn't dream of doing such things, because you have already entered the "Rat Race," and you have "Responsibilities."

Responsibilities: Also known as, "all that you do to continue possessing the stuff that keeps you tied down to wherever it is you are now." Oh, and just to put another bee in your bonnet-- you never really truly own anything. You are at best a temporary caretaker of anything you purchase; because, as we all know, you can't take it with you.

So, why spend your entire life gathering up useless things that you put in storage and continue paying for after you've "bought" it, if you can do nothing else with it but pass it on to the next generation, who most likely won't want it anyway? Seems like a terrible waste of time to me. Life is meant to be so much more than a mere shopping spree anyway.

Here is what I propose to all of you who have ventured this far with me: "Simplicity is Bliss;" do not acquire more than you can carry with you on any one trip. Keep it simple and lightweight. This way, you are free to blow with the wind and go wherever you please.

However, as I said before, this is merely a suggestion that most of you will not even dream of following. Therefore, I suggest this as a way of thinking, like Feng Shui for your life of acquisitions. Do not tie your self down so tightly that you are unable to take advantage of the opportunities that life throws at you. Open your mind to the possibility that at any moment you may be given a chance of a lifetime, and you must leave everything you own behind to move on to a new adventure.

Buy second hand furniture or used electronics. If you haven't used it in six months give it to the Goodwill. Lighten your load to lighten your life. "Simplicity is Bliss," my friends.

Don't get me wrong. Don't think that I'm getting all left-wing minimalist on you, and say you should burn your house and live in a tent. There is really nothing wrong with material possessions, nothing at all. New stuff is great! I love getting new clothes and toys. It makes you feel good to get new things.

We just have to make sure that we're not getting too caught up in the accumulation of these new things. You can buy and have as much as you want, as long as it doesn't keep you from really living your life. Those that have made themselves wealthy have more stuff than most of us can ever dream of, yet still live life on their terms and without restriction, because they have the means to do so and that is really the lesson here. Don't live beyond your means so much that you become a slave to your stuff.

It is better to have less and enjoy it more, than to have more and enjoy it less. You make your own choices and decisions about how this best fits and works for you, but a little tweaking and fine tuning would do us all good.

Now, this does not just apply to the material things in your life; it also applies to your life in general. Too many of us have decided to take every little piece of our lives so seriously, that at any moment we could make diamonds out of a lump of coal by placing the coal between our butt cheeks. There are so many people who are wound up so tight that they can snap at any moment, and often do--at the smallest and silliest things.

What is so important about your job, your home, or your

image that you have lost all the simple joys that life brings to others on a daily basis? Have you lost sight of the simple pleasures you had as a child? When was the last time you jumped into a puddle after a spring rain just to splash in the water and get wet? When was the last time you took a walk in the woods and actually looked up into the canopy of the trees instead of keeping your head down on the trail, worried you may get lost?

The greatest things in life are free. All you have to do is take a moment to enjoy them. Oh, and you don't need to buy anything to go out and enjoy them either. You can rent all the equipment you need, to explore and come back from your adventure.

We often worry way too much about the things that someone else has deemed important to us. It is not important to us, nor is it in the slightest bit necessary to us. It is, however, important to those making the commercials and selling the goods that you've been told you cannot live without. Take a look back a couple of chapters and get back in touch with you and what it is you truly want.

Once you stop listening to all that you see on TV or read in the newspapers, you'll start asking yourself what it is you really want and what makes you happy. Maybe it is the acquisition of more stuff; but stuff without someone to share it with really isn't all that much fun. So if you're going to spend your time getting more stuff, you should probably first find someone to share all that stuff with. Toys are no fun if you have to play with them by yourself.

Now, let me digress for a moment and reiterate a point to you: You must decide for yourself what is important to you, and what you want to spend your valuable time pursuing. I do not pretend to be able to comprehend even one-tenth of the possibilities there are for everyone in this world. But, I do understand a basic principle of happiness, which I have been sharing with you in several different ways throughout this book.

This principle is very basic and simple, as all the most powerful wisdoms are. Simplify your life. Or, if you prefer—live simply, so that others may simply live.

What is your definition of simplicity? What does the phrase, "Live simply", mean to you?

If you stop to look around you from time to time, you'll notice a growing trend in our society of "Too Much." We work "Too Much" to pay for "Too Many'" things that we don't need, which causes "Too Much" stress on us, which then leads to "Not Enough" happiness, which then eventually leads to disease and death.

What are you working so hard for? If it is not Happiness, Joy, and Love you are trying to provide, then I believe you are not listening to You, instead of what you have been told. You are listening to someone else's opinion and not your own.

The basic premise of this book is the power of your perceptions. What is guiding your perceptions? What standard of measure are you using when it comes to your perceptions? Do you perceive the world through your eyes or through someone else's?

The power of your perception can only be truly utilized when you are deciding for you. When you know what it is that you want and are working toward, then you can change your perceptions and effectively change your world as you know it.

Simple pleasure is just that, simple.

> *"To know life in every breath, in every cup of tea, in every moment. That is bushido. That is the way of the Samurai."*
>
> **(quoted from 'The Last Samurai')**

To be a Warrior in your life--for your life--you must retrain yourself to stop speeding through life unaware. Slow down and become aware and awakened to every aspect of life. Become aware of every moment, every breath, every smile, every laugh, and every kiss. Become aware of your perceptions. Make your awareness your perception and perception your awareness.

We run to and fro at the speed of sound on our quest; but a quest for what? What is it we seek, and how is it that we will ever find it when we are going too fast to catch any details from our surroundings? Speed is only a friend when the journey is meaningless. However, it is always the journey, and not the destination, that delivers the greatest lessons.

You must choose for yourself what your journey will be, and after choosing, you must take a step to begin your journey.

This is how life unfolds before us, whether we are conscious of it or not.

I say, "Simplicity is Bliss."

How would you phrase that same statement to fit you and your life? Begin with your own simple and easy phrase to define what you want out of life, and what you want your life to be. I cannot give it to you, because I am not you. You are you, and no other person knows what your heart truly desires.

I am merely here to give you some food for thought and some examples to inspire you on your way. You may take all that I say, half of what I say, a word or two here and there, or nothing at all of what I say to use in your life. The choice, as always, is yours.

But, I will say this to you again and again: "Simplicity is Bliss," because this truth has been true since the beginning of time and will hold true until the end. When you simplify your world into what is most important to you, then the rest becomes just a means to an end, and nothing to get bent out of shape over.

We, as complicated human beings, often have a knack for over-complicating things. We get so caught up in the smallest details and tiniest flaws that we never step back to take in the big picture and the perfection that is the world before us.

One simple answer is -- and how poetic that I am borrowing this from a movie: "find that one thing that is most important to you, and live for that."(City Slickers) What is that one thing that is most important to you? Is it your family? Is it your children? Is it your job? Is it your journey for truth? What is it?

Search your feelings and find the one thing that means the most to you in the world and go with that. Make that your main focus and let all the other stuff go.

When you simplify your life in this way it makes all those other things so small and insignificant that they will no longer affect you as they once did. You will feel stress free and happy again, as you let go of all that is unnecessary and focus solely on what means and matters most to you.

Try to choose that "one thing" that is most important to you. However, if you cannot choose just one thing, make yourself a list of the top ten most important things in your life, and categorize them from the least to the most important. Then live according to your list and new priority ranking of what is important to you.

I know, I hate lists too; I'm not the most organized person in the world and having to do all that organizing is, for me, like seeing my friendly neighborhood dentist for my next root canal. You just have to ask yourself: "How important is this to me? How important is it that I find my one thing so I can simplify my life and truly begin to enjoy it?"

The answer is there within you, you just have to find it. And, by all means, talk to friends and family. Get their input and ideas, but you are the one who has to make the final decision. You have to decide for you, because if anyone else did it for you, it really wouldn't be for you, now would it?

"Once more into the breach, my dear friends; once more into the breach!!"

It's off to war! I send you as warriors for life, love and happiness. Do not fear this war, but rejoice in it. Rejoice in the courage you are showing to break away and live life on your terms, for you. Become the warrior you were intended to be in this life, and take no prisoners as you venture forth to find your truth, and therefore, your life.

GOD BELIEVES IN YOU!

CHAPTER EIGHT

God believes in you, because God is you. God is that everlasting spark within you that gives you life. God is not some lonely man in the sky who looks down upon you in disappointment at the life you live. God loves you as we should try to love ourselves: unconditionally and with infinite patience.

There is no one person who can tell you what God is--no one knows for sure. But, I can tell you what I believe, and that is: God is all things. The energy that makes up all things is God. We, and everything else within and without this Universe, is God. God is the universal consciousness to which we belong, along with all other life forms in all the worlds and in all the galaxies of our Universe.

God knows, in every detail, everything that we know and experience, because we, as parts of God, experience it. There is no need to fear God, because that is the same as fearing yourself. If you do fear God or yourself, you are merely denying your own power to be the Great and Mighty Spiritual Being with Dignity, Direction, and Purpose that you truly are.

We should strive to live our lives fully and with love and joy, because that is how to truly honor God. By honoring yourself and owning the power within you to become and create any and all things that you desire in love and joy, you begin to truly know God. There is nothing in Heaven or on Earth that is unattainable to us, if we only believe and know that God is within us, giving us the power and purpose to realize all that we are.

You do not need to go to some church and make your ten percent tithe to be right in the eyes of God. God has no use for either churches or tithes, just as you have no need for these things. It is within each of us, in that spark that is us, that we will find God. Know thyself: and in doing so, you will know God.

God believes in you as God believes in him or herself. There is no need to fear or repent, for there is nothing worthy of either your fear or repentance. Lose those thoughts of a wrathful and vengeful God that we have been taught by the church; for God is neither, just as you are neither.

When your time to return home comes, who do you think will be there to judge you and the life you lived? If God wasn't available on that day to judge you, who would do the judging in God's place? If you had to stand in God's place on the day you return home to your natural spiritual self, what would you see, and how would you judge yourself? This is how you should live your life, not in fear of judgment from God, but in awe of your own judgment; for it will be you who will be reliving your life, and also living out how you affected others throughout your life, experiencing you through their eyes.

Imagine your Panoramic Life Review, as discussed earlier in this Book. The whole 'my life flashed before my eyes' thing, and not just you reliving every moment of your life again, but also re-living your interactions with all those people you came in contact with throughout your life; and feeling how you made those people feel. This is what we all have to look forward to when it is our time to step out of our little life experiment and back into our true spiritual selves, free from the physical bondage of our bodies.

Now, knowing that, how would you change things in your life now? If you knew that you would relive every experience again as you, and every person you came into contact with as well, what would you do differently? We are the only judge that we will ever really have to contend with; and if you're like me, I can be one hell of a hard-ass judge when it comes to myself. What will be your verdict? Will you find yourself guilty or innocent? What will be the charges you bring forth upon yourself?

Don't worry too much about it, because once you've left your body you will also leave behind all of those human hang-ups that you learned in this life, and will look upon the life you just lived as your true spiritual self, with unconditional love and kindness. You will see it for what it was; a journey of growth and exploration to further grow as a spiritual being. Oh, and if you were wondering, you can always come back and try again if you didn't accomplish what you set out for yourself in this lifetime. There is no such thing as a time limit on you; there really is no such thing as time or space anyway, so don't worry--you have time.

To clarify a little about something that I've always wondered about, and what I believe is pretty common to us all--let's look at what this life is for. What did God put us here to do? What is our purpose on this Earth, in this body, for this life?

What I've come to learn is this: Your purpose in this life is just that: life. To live your life as you see fit--in happiness, love and joy. God may have picked you to come down here in this body, but you made all the decisions and plans after that. You made a plan for what you wanted to do, learn, accomplish, and experience in this life. There is no one else but you when it comes to what the meaning of your life is. We are here to explore this physical world and live it, learn from it, and grow from the journey.

Once again, it comes back to you. You are the only judge you will ever stand before and you are the one who decided to come, here and now, to live this life. God wants nothing more than what you want for yourself. The question is: What do you want for yourself?

What is it that you are passionate about? What is it that you love more than anything else and would love to do for the rest of this life? Is it to be a mother or a father? Do you want to be a traveler and explore all that this beautiful world has to offer?

What do you want for you? Answer that question truthfully and honestly, and you will be one step closer to living a life full of joy, love and blissful happiness.

Round and round we go, and always, always, we come back to You. The heart of this whole thing is you; you being you, living for you, and loving you for you, and as you. God only wants for you what **you** want for you. Know it, believe it, and live it as God wishes. You came here to have a life so that God could experience it with you.

When you come to that place of understanding about who and what you truly are, and live your life in accordance with your own wishes, then you will come to know God. God is love, and love is the basis of **all** things. Everything comes from love, as everything comes from God; and so--everything comes from you.

Your power in this world is unfathomable and unending. The only thing that holds you back is you, and the belief that you are not a part of God living in a physical body upon this Earth. You are a Great and Mighty Spiritual Being with Dignity, Direction, and Purpose, and God knows this to be true as He/She wishes you would know it to be true. Do not hold yourself back from exploring the greatness that is You. Do not deny yourself because you believe that this is the way it is supposed to be, because society or something else told you it is that way. Search within yourself and you will know that you are without limit.

The potential of all humans has yet to be even touched upon.

All scientists will tell you that we only use about ten percent of our brains, and yet we have already accomplished so much. What do you think would happen if (will happen when) we all began to use one hundred percent of our brains? What wonders would (will) we experience? What kind of wonderful world would (will) we live in if (when) we all knew (know) and used (use) our full potential out of love and joy?

The thought itself is staggering to comprehend; but I truly believe that is what we are pushing toward and striving for. Let us all strive to explore our full potentials within these physical bodies. We can accomplish anything through the expressions of our full potential. Our greatest dreams will be realized and brought forth into this world as easily as we open a door or window, once we realize the capacity for greatness within ourselves.

Just as God is limitless so are we also, because we are all a part of God and have God-like ability within us just waiting to be tapped into and fully realized. This is the faith that is intended when speaking about faith in God; it is truly faith in ourselves as powerful spiritual beings of God living this physical reality.

If only it were that easy, Right? If only it were that easy to realize our full potential to create a Heaven on Earth. Well, who says it isn't?

Let us not forget that this world that we live in is an illusion. As an atom is only truly five percent "matter", only five percent of who and what we truly are can be within this physical time/

space reality. Only five percent of what you are is in the here and now. That leaves the other ninety-five percent of your true power untapped. You are truly God and are therefore of unlimited proportions. If you can accomplish all that you accomplish within this reality with just five percent of your true self focused here, imagine the possibilities if you tapped into the rest of you.

There is a world of unlimited possibilities awaiting all of us. It is up to us to search it out and find it within ourselves.

I would like to take a step back for a moment and try to relieve some of the pressure you may be feeling after finding out you are really God in a human suit. Try to remember as we go through all these lessons I've learned and am throwing at you: Time is an illusion. Everything that we experience on this Earth, in this time/space reality, is an illusion. You do not need to stress, rush, or worry that you need to realize your full potential and capabilities today, tomorrow, or next year. You don't even have to worry about doing it this lifetime or the next or the next. The truth is, you've most likely had hundreds or even thousands of lifetimes just to get this far. Take your time, because all that is and all that will be, will happen in its own due time; which is really funny, considering I just said time is an illusion.

All I mean is this: Because we only experience time from the physical reality perspective, we do not need to worry how long it will take or how much work we have to do to get there. There is no time, and there is no end to you or the work you are doing. You will continue on forever and you will never get it wrong because you will never get it done. Truthfully, there really is no "It" to get done. The process of living and learning is really the only "It" we need to be concerning ourselves with, because it is in the living and learning that the work gets done.

So, go forth my children, with love in your hearts and a spring in your step; for you are all God masquerading as humans upon this Earth. You have no responsibility at all, other than to live your life as you see fit, and to experience this journey that is life. Just remember to really live life as 'You' see fit, and not as someone else sees fit for you. All experience is good, and all experience is a lesson worth learning; especially the hard experiences, as they are the best teachers.

Hard lessons are the best--but I say it is best to learn from the hard lessons the first time, because who wants to go through that again? The thing is, and this is what I've learned through my own experiences in this life so far: We're all a bunch of knuckleheads who need to beat our heads against the wall a few millions times before we finally realize, "Hey, the wall is hard and my head hurts!"

Try to love yourself as God loves you, and be easier on yourself. Because, after all, you're only human (well, at least five percent of you is human and the rest is just waiting to rejoin that five percent when the time is right). But, again, time is an illusion and there is no time like now. That's all we really have any way--now. Try not to regret, or mourn the loss of the past, because it's gone; and the future is only a dream. Now is all we have. Let's make the best of it, and frickin' smile once in a while!! Because, if you aren't laughing, then you don't know God!

God loves you. Try to love yourself a little, too.

HELP YOURSELF BY GETTING OUT OF THE WAY!

CHAPTER NINE

As I'm sure you've discerned from all the previous chapters, the title of this chapter says it all. Help yourself -- by getting out of the way! What more needs to be said?

You probably guessed it, nothing more NEEDS to be said, but I just can't help myself. ☺

I am a writing fool; so I do as a writing fool does, and I go on--beating this poor old dead horse.

To truly grasp this concept of getting out of our way, we must grasp the fact that we have already chosen this life to lead, and set it up so that we may have the experiences we wanted to have in order to learn what lessons we wanted to learn. Your higher self, your true spiritual self, has set you up to succeed in this task. We just need to stop fighting it and go with it.

Most of us have forgotten why we came here in the first

place and have started running toward all the wrong things, simply because that is what we were told to do. It is no one's fault, really, because the ones who told us what we should be doing don't remember either. Not remembering is okay, and is pretty natural. Once we get here and start living in these bodies, we forget why we came--and it's in the remembering that the magic begins.

Remember the spark within you, your own personal piece of God, that which is the real you--not the flesh and bones bag that you reside in now. The real you has a plan and a mission, and it is up to you to figure out or remember what that plan is; and finding it out is not as hard as you may think. By letting go of what you've been taught here by society and others, and learning to follow your bliss, you will find yourself right back on track with all that you intended to do, learn, and be in this lifetime.

Following your bliss is as easy as figuring out what brings you joy and doing that. Enjoying whatever that may be, as much as you can, and as often as you can. When you find that one thing that is most important to you and that which brings you the most joy, you are in line with your Source and your truth. Nothing in this life should be hard or make you miserable if you live by and for that thing that you came here to do--that which makes you the most happy and joyful.

The problem is that we have forgotten and have all got caught up in the slave-like rat race of the "American Dream" that most of us are living for today. We toil and work our fingers to the bone, only to come home and feel unfulfilled, unsatisfied, and lost within ourselves. We ask, "There must be more than just this?" And there is; you just have to have a little faith in yourself and go for what you love.

This life was meant to be joyous and wonderful, not tedious and mundane. We do many things only because we think we have to, because that's what our parents did, and that is what everyone else is doing. It hasn't worked so well for them, so why do we follow suit? Mostly, I believe, it is because we don't remember who and what we really are. We relate only to this body, and we forget about our true spiritual selves. We forget about our power and our potential; and mostly, we forget that we can do or be anything we desire to be, and instead just relinquish ourselves to the so called "Norm."

When you get to know the real you, your true self--and start to get in line with what you planned to do in this lifetime-- you will begin to see the magic that is you as spirit, living as a human in this physical reality. You will begin to understand that you were meant to live a wondrously abundant life, full of joy and love. Forget what you have learned and seen as a human on this planet, and start to remember that you are so much more than that. Remember that you are a Great and Powerful Spiritual Being with Dignity, Direction, and Purpose. You are not just this skin suit, this bag of bones dragging yourself to your job and then home, just to do it all over again.

Once you begin to understand that this physical reality isn't all that real after all, that it is an illusion, created by us to learn our lessons and grow spiritually, you will begin to think differently and look at things differently. And, in truth, that is all you really need in order to gain a new, higher perspective of this life and you in it.

Take the pressure off yourself, because you don't need it. You don't need all those fancy things you see on TV. And to put it bluntly, you don't need to eat, drink or breathe because that body isn't you. You are the everlasting, eternal spiritual essence within that body and you are limited by nothing. You cannot die, you are eternal. Only the vessel can die. And yet it too does not die, but simply changes form and rejoins the earth, or is frozen, or embalmed, or mummified, or whatever. It is amazing all the weird things we do with our bodies. We grow so attached to them that we want to save them like all that old furniture you have in storage but don't use.

Just a little levity here to brighten the mood! Remember, if you're not laughing, you're not doing it right! Okay, let's get back to that dead horse again.

You are eternal. You are spirit. You are energy. You are energetic consciousness within a physical vessel. Period! The end!

Do not restrict yourself with thoughts of inadequacy, lack, or doubt. Release all that negativity and become what God meant for you to be: God spark in the flesh; all powerful and with unlimited potential. The only restrictions we have are those that we put on ourselves or learned from others. They are not natural for us.

Release those doubts, and release yourself to find yourself-- within your happiness and bliss. Stop fighting against your life just because that is all you have ever known. Break free and become the real you--happy, joyous, and loving.

We have all read, heard and learned it. It seems good in theory, but how do we do all that and still live in this physical time/space reality?

First get to know who and what you really are. One step at a time, one proverbial foot in front of the other--get to know the real you inside. Learn what you love, learn about your passions; learn about what you truly want to do in this life. Learn what makes you happy. Find that one thing that makes your gears go and your clock tick. I would love to tell you what that is, but I can't--you have to find it for yourself. There is help for you, as always, but you have to do most of the leg work.

It's not always easy either, because we do live in this time/space reality, and you want to keep up appearances of normality to avoid being stoned in the streets. Don't worry too much about that, though. There are more and more people waking up to their true selves and their true callings all the time; and they tend to migrate toward each other--forming groups and communities. Continue on your way, and let your life take you forward--like a great stream, toward your happiness. When you arrive there, you will find yourself surrounded by so many like-minded and open people, you will wonder what you did in that old life.

That is how it's supposed to go for us--life that is like a great and calm stream that will gently take us where we need to go, if we just let go of the oars and stop fighting it. Yet most of us are fighting it, however; and if you take a look around you at all those that are fighting the flow of life, you'll see a lot of stressed out people. I mean really, have you ever tried to paddle upstream in a good size river? It takes a lot of hard work just to stay where you are.

Fall into the flow of life and let it take you where it will. You have already made your itinerary, and have mapped out the way; all you have to do is just let go and the river will take you. Just sit back, relax, and enjoy the ride. Take a look around and enjoy the sights and sounds of your journey; but don't try to turn back upstream, because that's not a battle you can win, my friend.

Now, more about that stream. You may be asking yourself, "What stream? How do I let go and go with the flow if I don't know what stream or river I am in?" That is a very good question. Let's go back to what makes you happy. What is it in this world that gives you purpose and makes you the happiest? That is really all you need to figure out. And once you do, the rest will start to fall into place.

The thing is, whatever your passion, it will be different for you than anyone else, and that is by design. The wonderful thing about our life, and this world we live in, is that we don't all want or desire the same things. There will never be a shortage of things or happiness for us if we follow our hearts and our bliss. Whatever it is you truly love and desire to do may be similar to others, but never exactly the same. That is why you never need to worry about lack or not enough; there is more than enough to go around for everyone.

The lack that we feel is in many ways an indicator that we haven't found our path and place yet. That we lack is also a clever message instilled by those that want us to spend our money on their product, telling us we must rush to get that new thing before they are all gone.

Happiness is free, dear people, you just have to go find yours and own it. Don't let others tell you what will make you happy, because they don't have a clue as to what will make you happy. That is your job to find and to hold. By all means, talk to others and get ideas, but never rely on another's opinion to make your own final decision. You are you, living for you, and your happiness. No one else can give that to you or take it away if you don't let them.

What does this all mean? You will have to figure that out for yourself. Just know that if it feels right, it is. And if it feels wrong, it is. Learn who you are and what you truly desire in this world, and let nothing stop your forward momentum.

I do have one word of caution: Make sure you get to the root of you, and work through all the stuff that has been imbedded into you and your space by others and this world, before deciding which way you go. Many of us need to figure out what our hang ups and neuroses are, and work through them first before we can take honest stock of what it is that we most want in this life. A clue, if the thought starts with "I should" or "ought to," it's one of those. Recognize it as someone else's plan for you and get rid of it.

I know that for me, in particular, I've had to work through

a lot of personal demons before I could begin to know myself and what I wanted to do with this life. It wasn't always easy, and by no means am I finished yet. This Book, and all the hours and years of self exploration and inner searching, are the tools for me in my growth and progress. I am not done, and as stated before, I will never be done, because we never finish growing and creating. We are eternal creators and growers. We will never finish; and therefore, we can never get it wrong. All that we experience just takes us closer to the next step in our spiritual evolutionary ladder.

Rejoice in your growth processes, rejoice in all that life is and can be. Do not let yourself be waylaid by a rough patch or hard times in your life, for those are our greatest teachers and our greatest periods of growth. As hard as those times are, you can make them so much more bearable by remembering that: **"This, too, shall pass; and you will be that much better and stronger because of it."**

Find the self within yourself, my friends; and rejoice in this life and in your journey. Joy and happiness are just a thought and a slight change of perspective, away. Decide to be happy every day, for no reason at all, and you will be. Be like a child again; because children are always happy and need a reason to despair. Many of us have forgotten this, and are in despair and need a reason to be happy. Happiness is its own reason and its own reward. Decide to be happy for yourself, and as yourself, and the rest will just fall away and lose its hold on you.

Yes, this will take some practice as well, but once you have felt happy -- just because you decided to be happy -- you will realize that it really isn't as hard as it sounds. Your mind is your most powerful tool, and happiness is just a thought away. Think of your kids, your pets, your family, or anything else that makes you happy. Hold that feeling for as long as you have time; then do it again tomorrow for a longer period of time, and then again, and again, and again. The more you do this, the more you will put yourself in tune with who and what you really are, and the more in the flow of your stream you will be.

It really isn't all that hard to find happiness and joy in life. All you need to do is make the choice to be happy and joyful. Once you have made that choice, God, the Universe, and your true self will help show you the way. Decide for yourself, for your own good, that starting today; you will be happy for no good reason at all--just because you want to be happy. Make the world try to make you unhappy. Be stubborn and hardheaded about it. Announce to the world that you are happy and there is nothing it can do about it. Make a game of it and really enjoy it. Smile yourself all the way to the Bank of Bliss and let the rest of the world follow suit; because if they can't beat you, they'll just have to join you.

So, get out of your own way and be happy--just because you want to, and because you deserve to be. Let no man put asunder what you have created today, and you will know bliss.

You are Great and Mighty Spiritual Beings with Dignity, Direction, and Purpose. You don't have to pretend to be or try to be--you already are. You just need to know it, believe it, hold it, and get out of your own way and just **be it.**

God bless you and yours.
You bless you and yours.
I bless you and yours.

SO, WHAT DOES THIS ALL MEAN FOR YOU?

CHAPTER TEN

So, what does this all mean for you? Hmmm, that's a tough one. I think I'll have to defer to the expert on that subject: You.

So, Mr. or Ms. Expert, what does this all mean for you? What have you learned from the words, ideas and concepts you've just read? What are you taking away from it?

Like most teachers, I can only present information. I try to make it as easy and simple as possible, and hope that you will understand what you need. You must decide what makes the most sense to you; what you will use, and what you will choose to discard.

For me, and possibly for many of you, it comes down to simply putting all these concepts into your own perspective, and defining them in a way that best suits you. The key to any new principle or way of thinking is to make it your own, and own it as if you created it; it is your new baby.

All of the concepts I have provided for you in this book are not my own. These are the things I have learned, and am still learning. I have put them here for you in my own words and thoughts in hopes of explaining some enormously complicated concepts, in an easy-to-understand way. For me, that has always worked the best—to cut away all the fat and frilly cover up and get to the heart of the issue. Decide what it means for me, and use it in a way that best fits my life.

This is what I am suggesting for you. Take it, make it your own, and use it how you see fit. You are the boss--the power is in your hands. I have led you to the water. You may drink your fill or go thirsty. I will stifle the urge to push the horse's head into the water and make him drink. It wouldn't work, anyway. As humans, we sometimes would rather drown than to do what someone said would be "good for" us. TELL ME I'M WRONG! ☺

What everything I've said means is simple: This is your life to live however you see fit, and in whatever fashion makes you the happiest. That's all anyone wants of you, and all anyone can ask. Be yourself; live as yourself, and be happy as yourself. Be the best YOU that you can be.

The most important thing I can impart to you is this: Your perspective shapes your world. Your perspective in this world, and in this life, is everything. Your perspective is what makes you, you--and what helps you decide what is important to you and what isn't. Having a joyful perspective on life as the wondrous spiritual being you are, living in this human experience, is an amazing way to go through life.

Your perspective can make mountains out of molehills, and something out of nothing. Or, it can make nothing out of something, and atoms out of atom bombs. It's all in how you look at your world and what is important in it to you.

There is no easier, faster, or more complete way to change your life for the better, in a split second, than to change your perspective. Focus on what is truly important to you. When you know what matters to you most in life, the rest becomes trivial. Don't give away your power to others by falling into those old habits of judgment and reaction. Give yourself the permission to be happy for no reason at all, and let the rest worry about themselves.

You have the power to create the most wonderful world you can imagine, here and now. Take that power and own it. Be who you've always wanted to be. Be you. Stop trying to be someone else, because that won't get you where you really want to be. That can only hold you back from the amazing person you really are, and that you and God intended you to be.

The happiest people on Earth are not the richest or most powerful people that we see on television. They are the people who know who and what they are, and rejoice in being themselves everyday. That is all we were meant to be. You are perfect and powerful, just as you are. Love yourself as God loves you and you will see that love and bliss will be revisited upon you a thousand fold.

That is what all of this means to me. I hope that in time, it will mean the same for you.

EPILOGUE

Thank you, thank you, and thank you again for sticking with me through this journey we've taken together. Thank you, also, for taking the time to read the words I've written. I feel honored and blessed that you would spend some of your valuable time with me and my book.

I hope you have taken something away from it that is helpful, and I hope you will return as often as you like to take something else from the information contained within these pages. The process of writing this book has been an awesome and awakening journey for me. There is a saying that we teach what we most need to learn. I began my learning and wanted to share my knowledge. In preparing to do so, I learned so much more. If you got something you needed from what I had to say, watch for my next book because I still have a lot to learn to become my best Me. ☺

Try to love all those that enter your life, because the most amazing teachers come in the most unconventional packages; and you never know what you may learn from the most unlikely sources. If you have children, open up your hearts and your minds to them, because they are some of the greatest life teachers one could ever hope for. Try to remember that their lack of age only means that they are that much closer to the Source of all things, and their purity of thought and intellect have powerful lessons if you only grant yourself the eyes to see them.

Above all, be true to yourself. Be kind and gentle with yourself. Stop punishing yourself for mistakes you've made or martyring yourself to others. That only holds you back from the love and happiness that you deserve. We tend to be our own worse critics and are usually a hundred times harder on ourselves than anyone else would be. Have patience with yourself as much as you have for others; and remember that this is all a learning process. What we consider to be a failure is really a wonderful lesson in disguise.

Thomas Edison is paraphrased as saying that he did not fail two thousand times while trying to invent the light bulb, but rather learned two thousand ways not to make a light bulb.

That is a wonderful way of looking at life and our lessons in it. Be kind to yourself during this learning process. How long must we go on learning? If you're still alive, you are still learning.

I love you all, and thank you.

CPSIA information can be obtained
at www.ICGtesting.com
Printed in the USA
FSOW01n0012280115
4821FS